witness

Learning to Tell the Stories of Grace
That Illumine Our Lives

"Here is a rich resource for anyone seeking to pass on the faith with clarity and conviction—whether in the pulpit, in the classroom, or in daily life. *Witness* reminds us of the power in our stories and offers tools for telling them in ways that convey God's grace at work in our lives. Leonard DeLorenzo is a gifted storyteller himself and makes us eager to put his ideas to work. What a blessing this will be to so many!"

Deacon Greg Kandra
Catholic blogger and journalist

"Incorporating 'stories of grace' in catechesis, sacramental preparation, youth and young adult ministry, retreats, and theology classes is a powerful way to pass on the faith as a living and dynamic reality, an encounter with the true God who is not an unknown, impersonal deity but the God who showed us his face in Jesus Christ. He enters into our lives and speaks to us as truth, beauty, goodness, mercy, and love. Leonard DeLorenzo teaches us to form disciples who are able to see God's grace in their lives, and, like Pope Francis, discover their identity as persons 'looked upon by the Lord.' This book will help readers bring their formation efforts to a whole new level, leading to a deeper and more personal engagement with the mysteries we teach—most importantly, the mystery of God who touches our lives with his grace."

Most Rev. Kevin C. Rhoades
Bishop of Fort Wayne-South Bend

"This unique resource helps Catholics of all ages witness to their faith by sharing with their families, neighbors, and colleagues 'stories of grace'—ways God is acting in their everyday lives."

Sr. Theresa Rickard, O.P.
President of RENEW International

"Many concerned Catholics are working hard to reconsider how to re-evangelize Catholic young people faithfully and effectively. Leonard DeLorenzo is one of the best I know who is devoted to this challenge. I highly recommend this book as an important contribution to the larger conversation."

Christian Smith
Coauthor of *Young Catholic America*

"The bad news is that emerging adults are leaving the Church. The good news is that Leonard DeLorenzo has written a remarkable and well-researched book full of personal stories about how the lost art of storytelling can bring them back. Telling one's story in front of others can be uncomfortable, but it can also work miracles. DeLorenzo has decades of experience forming disciples by helping them to move beyond clichés and sound bites to identify the messy work of grace in their lives."

Anna Nussbaum Keating
Coauthor of *The Catholic Catalog*

witness

Learning to Tell the Stories of Grace
That Illumine Our Lives

LEONARD J. DELORENZO

Ave Maria Press AVE Notre Dame, Indiana

Founded in 1865, Ave Maria Press is a ministry of the United States Province of Holy Cross.

www.avemariapress.com

Paperback: ISBN-13 978-1-59471-687-4

E-book: ISBN-13 978-1-59471-688-1

Cover design by Angela Moody, amoodycover.com.

Text design by Christopher D. Tobin.

Printed and bound in the United States of America.

Library of Congress Cataloging-in-Publication Data
Names: DeLorenzo, Leonard J., author.
Title: Witness: learning to tell the stories of grace that illumine our
   lives / Leonard J. DeLorenzo.
Description: Notre Dame, Indiana: Ave Maria Press Inc., 2016. | Includes
   bibliographical references. | Description based on print version record
   and CIP data provided by publisher; resource not viewed.
Identifiers: LCCN 2016030227 (print) | LCCN 2016022587 (ebook) | ISBN
   9781594716881 () | ISBN 1594716889 () | ISBN 9781594716874 (pbk.) | ISBN
   1594716870
Subjects: LCSH: Witness bearing (Christianity) | Storytelling--Religious
   aspects--Christianity. | Storytelling in Christian education. | Spiritual
   formation. | Christian life--Catholic authors.
Classification: LCC BV4520 (print) | LCC BV4520.D425 2016 (ebook) | DDC
   248/.5--dc23
LC record available at https://lccn.loc.gov/2016030227

To the Notre Dame Vision Mentors-in-Faith
You are the ones the light shines through

Contents

Introduction
The Stories We Tell Each Other

I tend to leave my car radio set to just one station, which happens to be the local affiliate of National Public Radio. Since my short daily commute is pretty regular, the timing of my drive home often coincides with the national broadcast of *Marketplace*, a business program that reports on the economic ramifications of all the day's news. In those few minutes spent in my car, I hear about how a conflict in one corner of the globe or a drought in another affects a supply chain, flusters investors, or paradoxically increases both optimism and panic in the global market. Though the amount of time I spend listening on any given day is never long, hearing short segments from this show over the span of a number of years has trained me not only to become a more attuned audience member but also to reflexively think about the economic implications of major world events whenever I hear about them, whether during this show or otherwise. Regularly listening to stories crafted from this certain perspective and for this certain purpose subtly but surely changes the way I perceive and think about what is happening in the world.

Of course, this show is neither the only nor even a major means by which I perceive and think about the world, and I am not attempting to critique what this show does or how it does it. What I do want to confess is that I have come to recognize how the stories we tell each other influence our views of the world around us. In this case, I sometimes find myself thinking first of all in terms of what is good for the global economy and measuring the positive or negative aspects of the news against this standard. If this were the one and only show I ever listened to, and if I listened to it all the time, it would be exceedingly difficult for me to conceive of world events in any manner other than through the economic causes and consequences of these events or to measure "good" and "bad" news in any other way. While I am not at all in danger of becoming a full-time, nonstop listener of this radio broadcast or of financial news in general, I am prompted to wonder about how the stories we tell each other train us to perceive and think.

It turns out that I am not alone in wondering about this. One of Max Lucado's best-known books is on this very subject, a children's book titled *You Are Special*. A race of wooden people spends all day, every day, giving each other star stickers and dot stickers to measure each person's perceived value in the community. If you can do something powerfully, confidently, or boisterously, you get a star, just as you would if your wooden skin were smooth or well polished or just the right shade. If you are clumsy or unsure of yourself or if you are in any way unpleasing to others, you get a dot. Most of the wooden people have both stars and dots, while a few are covered with just stars and an even more sizable minority are covered with only dots. Unsurprisingly, those with more stars than dots become more self-assured and accrue even more praise from the community, while those whose dots outnumber their stars tend to perpetually lose esteem not only in the eyes of others but also in terms of how they see themselves. In very explicit terms, *You Are Special* acknowledges that the standards we use to measure things—especially people!—matter, as do the stories we tell each other that communicate those values and give them currency. The underlying concern in this simple children's tale is the question about what counts as an accurate view of the world.

Following this logic, C. S. Lewis, in *The Silver Chair*, pits disparate views of the world in opposition to one another, with each claiming to provide the accurate picture. Toward the end of the tale, a couple of children and a creature native to the land of Narnia finally find the kidnapped prince for whom they have been searching throughout the story. The queen of the Underworld is holding him captive underground, where she has cast a spell over him to make him forget that he ever lived above ground. In order to free him, the members of the search party must not only help the prince to remember that there is a world beyond the small, dark cave in which he has been held captive but also keep themselves open to the larger world from which they came but cannot at present see. The queen's tactic is to lull them into agreeing with the interpretation of the world that she provides, where everything is contained in what they presently see. The queen offers one explanation after another about how everything they think they remember from the outside is merely a fanciful elaboration on what they see in the place where they currently abide. The queen's effort is in fact to make her audience into full-time, nonstop listeners who lose the ability to conceive of the world in any terms other than her own. Their liberation hangs upon being able to remember and trust in other stories besides the one the queen spins in her spell.

A similar kind of drama takes place but from the other direction in another famous children's story: *The Velveteen Rabbit*. The rabbit begins in a sort of existence where being unreal appears by most manners of reckoning totally closed to other possibilities. In short order, though, the rabbit hears a story from the Skin Horse that points toward the all-but-unbelievable possibility of inanimate playthings becoming real through the love of a child. Whereas the queen of the Underworld seeks to take the open possibilities of the "overworld" and confine them to the small measurements of the "underworld" where she alone reigns, the Skin Horse implants the seed of hope within the Velveteen Rabbit that the possibility of an open future exists beyond the closed fate of an unreal object destined ultimately for being discarded. In either case, the underlying logic is consistent: the stories we tell each other have power—for good or for ill—and the way in which we measure good and ill hangs in the balance with the what, how, and why of these stories.

From the simple wisdom of children's book authors and the sophisticated analyses of financial experts, I have learned the importance of the kind of stories we tell each other. While it is true that the world is what the world is and we are what we are, it is also true that the ways in which we tell the stories of the world and of ourselves is much more an open question than a settled issue. If all the news of the events of the day may be told from a primarily economic perspective, they may also be told from the perspective ecological causes and consequences or the perspective of human dignity measured in some manner or other. The exchange of star stickers and dot stickers only makes sense if we either consciously or subconsciously assent to the whole system of measuring value upon which that particular economy exists. In the starkest terms, the world either squashes or invites our wonder, but whichever one we think is accurate depends very much on the way in which we are willing to see the world. What interests me is learning to see the world in God's light, specifically through the practice of crafting and telling what I will call "stories of grace."

This book emerges from both a sense of gratitude and a sense of mission. I am grateful that for more than a decade stories of grace have surrounded me on a regular basis, primarily through my work with the Notre Dame Vision program. In my role as director of this program, I have guided hundreds of college students as they crafted stories of grace from their own lives to share with the high school participants of our annual summer conferences. These stories—offered in trust and as acts of faith—have helped me, along with countless others, to see the world, other people, and myself first and foremost in the light of God's mercy. My gratitude for all of the Notre Dame Vision Mentors-in-Faith is immense, and so it is to them that I dedicate this book.

Several of those former mentors generously agreed to share pieces of their stories of grace in chapter 3, so I owe a special debt of gratitude to Ashley Scott, Emma Fleming, Vincent David, Sarah Ruszkowski, Renée Roden, Geoffrey Burdell, Victoria Kay, Katlyn Patterson, and Dr. Timothy O'Malley as well as Stephanie DePrez, who allowed me to represent two of her stories in chapter 4. I am likewise filled with gratitude for the following colleagues in Notre Dame Vision with whom I have had the privilege of working to guide our mentors in crafting their stories of grace year after year: Megan Shepherd; Scott Boyle; Aimee Shelide Mayer; Mary Kate Radelet; Dave Ballintyn; Luke Slonkosky; Father Dan Parrish, C.S.C.; Father Pete McCormick, C.S.C.; and Father Pat Reidy, C.S.C.

I know the importance of good mentoring and faithful guidance in crafting stories of grace because when I myself was a Vision Mentor, my predecessors on the leadership team of Notre Dame Vision helped me craft a story of grace to share with the high school participants of yesteryear. My gratitude thus extends to the founding director of Notre Dame Vision, Steve Camilleri; the first two assistant directors, Sheila Provencher Abdallah and Dr. Nicole Shirilla, MD; the program's original designer and theological educator, Dr. Jan Poorman; and last but certainly not least, my boss and the leader of the McGrath Institute for Church Life, without whom, for so many reasons, none of this work would be possible: Dr. John Cavadini.

The sense of mission that gives rise to this book follows from the recognition that crafting and sharing stories of grace is a practice in learning to see all things not only as they should be but also as they truly are. "The Word became flesh and dwelt among us" (Jn 1:14, RSV) to reveal the truth of who God is, who we are, and how the mercy of Jesus Christ forges the bonds of communion across all forms of separation, isolation, and fear. To tell our stories of grace is to allow *the* Word to use our words to heal wounds and inspire hope. Stories of grace bring good news in excess of the capacities held

xvi   Witness

by clichés, platitudes, and general assumptions. As a practice, this form of storytelling—specific and limited as it is—responds to the needs of persons growing in faith, wavering in faith, and searching for faith alike, presenting a vision of the world in which God draws near to redeem and save. In the prevalent modern culture, we have become more comfortable with status updates, witty quips, quick chats, tweets, and retweets than with the basic human practice of storytelling; the time has come to reclaim our gift for storytelling and to reclaim it as a means of evangelization. This book arises from the mission of the new evangelization in seeking to identify the faith-formation issues of our times, propose a strategic response to these issues, and then provide substantive resources for instituting this strategic response through more regular practice.

With the energy of gratitude become mission, I hope that what follows will help strengthen disciples and those who form disciples in boldly announcing the wonder of the Lord's mercy from every nook and cranny of our lives. As we will see, stories of grace always deal with concrete particularities because the personal nature and intensity of God's love in Jesus Christ deems no one too small, no experience too peculiar, for becoming a beacon of light for the world. In response to God's confidence in us, let us never tire of wrapping ourselves in the stories of his love and entrusting ourselves to him who is worthy of all praise:

> Praise the LORD!
> Praise, O servants of the LORD,
>   praise the name of the LORD!
> Blessed be the name of the LORD
>   from this time forth and for evermore!
> From the rising of the sun to its setting
>   the name of the LORD is to be praised!
> The LORD is high above all nations,
>   and his glory above the heavens!

Who is like the LORD our God,
    who is seated on high,
who looks far down
    upon the heavens and the earth?
He raises the poor from the dust,
    and lifts the needy from the ash heap,
to make them sit with princes,
    with the princes of his people.
He gives the barren woman a home,
    making her the joyous mother of children.
Praise the LORD!

—Psalm 113 (RSV)

Chapter 1

The Light by Which We See

The Problem and Promise of Identity

If someone were to call you by name and ask, "Who are you?" how would you respond? It is an unsettling question because having to say one thing about the whole of your existence is daunting. Each of us knows a lot about ourselves, while at the same time, most of us also know that there is a lot about ourselves that we do not understand. To define yourself in one way comes at the expense of defining yourself in other ways, and no one likes to be limited. Even more disturbing is the occasional realization that "I may not really know myself at all." This problem of identity exists for each of us, no less for those who claim to be disciples. And it was precisely this question that an interviewer asked Jorge Mario Bergoglio shortly after he took the name Francis. After a period of thinking and searching for the right words and the right image, the new pope responded in the manner of a disciple: "I am one who is looked upon by the Lord."[1]

The disciple sees himself as one who is first of all seen; the disciple knows himself first of all as one who is known. This is a fascinating little paradox: that the way a disciple identifies himself is, first and foremost, to recognize that he is identified by another—namely, the Lord. Not unlike the rest of us, Pope Francis was aware of the various traits he possessed and the different things he knew about himself—such as that he is "a bit astute" and "really, really

1

undisciplined"—but he also knew that not one of these things or even the whole collection of them could account for who he is. All these other things abide within the one truly necessary thing: the Lord looks upon him in love. He knows himself as one seen in this way, and the whole story of who he is exists within the project of coming to believe, ever more fully, that this is true. A disciple sees in response to being seen and knows in response to being known.

In the pope's imagination, Caravaggio's painting of *The Calling of Saint Matthew* expresses the paradox of the disciple's identity. The moment the artist portrays is one in which all of the agency belongs to Jesus. On his initiative alone, Jesus looks upon Levi, who will become Matthew, in the midst of his typical crowd and engaged in his typical tax-collecting activities. Levi is stunned, awestruck even, as he raises his own finger to himself as if to confirm that Jesus is in fact pointing toward him. The rest of the scene is held in suspended animation—for this decisive moment, there is no movement. Two of Levi's companions remain engaged in their previous endeavors, while the other two look up to observe this interruption. Connecting the two sides of the canvas is the beam of light running along Jesus' outstretched hand and following his gaze onto Levi. In the dawn of this new light, Levi is called forth into Matthew and his identity is established: Matthew is the one whom the Lord looks upon. The story of Matthew begins here, and from this moment all the stories he had previously lived are recast in light of the Lord looking upon him. In the light of the Lord's mercy, Matthew begins to see himself and all things new. Contemplating this image helped Francis to see himself accordingly.

Francis could have just as easily invoked the subject of another one of Caravaggio's paintings: Saint Thomas the Apostle. In this painting, Caravaggio ponders the scene in the twentieth chapter of John's gospel, where the Lord shows his wounds to Thomas, who is coming to believe in the Resurrection as he sees. The evangelist brings the episode to a close with Jesus' words: "Blessed are those who have not seen and have believed" (Jn 20:29). Because of the Lord's words, we might suppose there is some easier route to belief that comes by way of seeing directly but that most of us, like Pope Francis and unlike Saint Thomas and Saint Matthew, are destined to struggle along the more difficult path of coming to believe without seeing. It seems that the goal is to believe whether or not one sees, whether by easier or harder means. But if we are too quick in assuming we know why Saint Thomas passed over from seeing to believing when the risen Christ came to him bodily, then we miss what and how Thomas actually saw. Thomas doesn't just see wounds, a body, and a person—he sees "my Lord and my God" (20:28). In that shift from seeing a stranger to seeing who this really is standing before him, Thomas sees *himself* as the one to whom the Risen One has offered peace. He had been looking for verification to placate his mind, but he ends up seeing himself as known, loved, and desired. *His* way of seeing yielded to *God's* way of seeing in Christ. In that sense, Thomas didn't stop seeing but rather started seeing by the light of God. In short, he believed.[2]

In his book on the theology of transformation, Bishop Robert Barron declares from the outset that "Christianity is, above all, a way of seeing."[3] This is inarguably true, but only in the sense that the Christian way of seeing is born of and responds to God's way of seeing us. Of course, it would be delightful if one could all of a sudden pass over into seeing oneself according to the mercy of the Lord. The fact is, however, that a mark of our fallen nature is our inability or unwillingness to see ourselves in this way. In response to this blindness, the Lord lends us his sight: when the Lord looks upon us in mercy, the redemption from our blindness begins, and as we learn to see in this light, we become who we are called to be. Initiating, educating, and guiding others into this belief and response is the work of Christian formation. The fruits of the long work of formation become evident when, in response to the question, "Who are you?" one is able to respond, "I am one who is looked upon by the Lord." This is the starting point for the story of a Christian life.

Enabling others to shape their life as a Christian story is the aim of Christian formation, and so this book is about Christian formation, but it isn't about *all* of Christian formation. More specifically, I am interested in highlighting a singular and demanding practice that promotes integrated faith formation in a way that is at once timeless and specially suited to the present day. The practice we will explore together is that of crafting and sharing "stories of grace." In naming "grace" as central to the kind of storytelling I will propose, I am interested in the ways in which one learns to translate one's own stories according to the presence of grace, which one must first learn to see. When I speak of "stories," then, I do not have in mind the more or less definitive conversion stories that are especially revered within certain Christian communions. Instead, I am talking about something much humbler: those shorter, oftentimes simple, intentionally contained stories of particular experiences, relationships, obstacles, sufferings, joys, and even epiphanies by which those whom the Lord has looked upon have begun learning to see themselves—and, in some way, the world—in *God's* light.

Learning to craft and tell these more particular kinds of stories is ordered to the lifelong task of learning how to tell one's whole story as a response to the Lord's look of love. The wisdom of the Christian formation germane to Catholicism in particular is that we can trust smaller practices in more ordinary things to lead, in the end, to the holistic transformation God intends for us. Over time and with practice, we learn how to cooperate with the work the Lord has already begun in us (see Phil 1:6).

Therefore, the kind of stories upon which we will focus is familiar to many, whether from retreats, youth conferences, or even parish missions. For those who have experience guiding youth and young adults in crafting and sharing "retreat talks" or "witness talks" on various topics, I hope that what I offer in the pages to follow contributes to a collegial conversation among fellow ministers and educators for the good of those to whom we minister and for the good of the Church. For those pastoral ministers, religious educators, and theology teachers who may not have much (if any) experience incorporating the practice of crafting and sharing stories such as these in ministry and teaching settings, I hope to propose a new possibility that fosters growth in knowledge, understanding, and love of the faith. And for those adults who, like myself, continue to work on living our lives as faithful disciples, I hope that together we can accept the challenge to become more reflective about, articulate with, and courageous in claiming the ways in which the Lord's loving gaze illumines our lives.

To set our bearings in regard to the more practical issues that I will take up in the subsequent chapters pertaining to the practice of actually crafting stories and the various uses for them, I want to devote some time in this chapter to examining the two main features of this approach to faith formation. On the one hand, we need to deeply consider the "mystery of grace" and to allow our imaginations to grow as the Lord beckons. On the other hand, we need to account for why exactly storytelling is so important. We will take up these two tasks in short order, but before doing so I want to dwell a little longer on the urgent question of identity. In particular, I want to recognize how this is the most urgent and relevant question for the generation most likely to leave the Church and, therefore, how it is also an incomparably important question for engaging the disengaged (or the rapidly disengaging) within the mission of the new evangelization.

Emerging Adults and God in Everyday Life

The biggest difference between twenty-three to twenty-eight-year-old Americans who identify as Catholic and those who identify as former Catholics is the belief that "God is a personal being involved in the lives of people today" (58.82 percent of Catholics to 33.47 percent of former Catholics).[4] There are numerous other differences of course, such as time spent praying alone and the frequency of parents attending religious services, but the largest discrepancy pertains to the issue of the personal nature of God and God's investment in everyday life.

Jeffrey Arnett describes this age group as the "emerging adults" who are distinct from both adolescents and adults, including young adults. "Emerging Adulthood is not a universal part of human development," Arnett explains, "but a life stage that exists under certain conditions that have occurred only quite recently and in some cultures."[5] This stage of life occurs where there is a "gap of at least several years between the time young people finish secondary school and the time they enter stable adult roles in love and work."[6] During this in-between period that has become more and more prevalent in recent decades, Arnett recognizes five traits common to these twentysomethings that, together, distinguish them from other groups: a sense of instability, a predominant self-focus, a sense of being in transition, a sense of general optimism, and, first and foremost, a sense of identity exploration. Emerging adulthood ends when people "settle down" and the habits formed during this indeterminate time crystallize into a determinate way of life.

Focusing on emerging adults is important because, even though this stage of life is distinct and by definition temporary, it is not isolated from other stages of life. While those passing through this period may think and act as if what happens in your twenties stays in your twenties, the fact of the matter is that what happens in your twenties leads to who you become in your thirties, forties, and beyond.[7] Moreover, the habits, behaviors, and dispositions that one brings into the in-between phase of "emerging adulthood" come from the preceding stages of life—namely, childhood and adolescence. Therefore, to truly focus on the needs of those in this critical stage of identity exploration, we must expand our vision to include both the formation of younger people who will soon pass through this period and those adults who, from beyond this stage, model adulthood for those coming after them and who also directly educate the young, whether through teaching, ministering, mentoring, or, most especially, parenting.

On the basis of his now well-known study on the religious and spiritual lives of teenagers, Christian Smith argues that the default religious identity of American teens is "moralistic therapeutic deism." This religious posture is composed of a loose set of tenets, all of which mimic Christian doctrine in a generic fashion. The operative notion of God that functions in this implicit belief system is what Smith describes as "Divine Butler" or "Cosmic Therapist."[8] God stands at the ready to take care of problems that arise in one's life, helping people to feel better about themselves, but otherwise God is not personally involved in the workings of the world. Rather than simply a stage through which young people pass, Smith further argues that this religious disposition is at once a "mirror" of the society that is forming the younger generation and a "barometer" of what will be the religious disposition of future adults—that is, the adults these young people will become.[9] In terms of serving as a mirror of society at large and of their elders in particular, Kenda Creasy Dean posits that these dumbed-down notions of God are not the result of the inadequate communication of religious belief from one generation to the next but rather indicative of very successful communication. Dean argues that adults are effectively passing on the unsubstantial religious identity that they themselves have settled into, so that "young people practice Moralistic Therapeutic Deism not because they reject Christianity, but because this is the only 'Christianity' they know."[10]

If young people are entering into the crucial period of identity exploration with vague notions of God and unsubstantial religious identity, then they are very likely to leave that phase of indeterminacy with a quite determinate belief that God is not personally involved in their own lives or in the world. Through the period of emerging adulthood, inchoate beliefs and assumptions harden while skills, capacities, and incapacities settle into place and form the foundation of adult life. I am not hereby suggesting that once someone turns thirty, there is no longer any hope of evangelization or catechesis, but I am arguing that the kind of character that has developed by the end of emerging adulthood is either more or less conducive to living a life of faith and of allowing one's own life story to be told as a Christian story.

Baseball coaches do not wait until players are becoming professionals to teach them the proper mechanics of a swing, and music teachers do not wait until pianists are preparing for concerts before making them practice scales. Professional hitters begin to develop the skills and habits of a good swing long before they enter the big leagues, while concert pianists' decades of practice are hidden within the masterful performances of their later years. Taking a long view of Christian formation will lead to analogous approaches: to begin by thinking about the kind of adult Catholics we want to form and then intentionally orienting our formation efforts at every stage to that end. From another perspective, we might think about what we want children to learn from their parents and then work to intentionally form parents (and future parents) toward that quality of faith. In either case, the plan for Christian formation must be comprehensive rather than piecemeal, meaning that whatever we hope to find at the end of emerging adulthood must also shape how we form both younger Catholics and adult Catholics.

While there are numerous skills and capacities that teenagers seem to lack in terms of developing a substantive religious identity, Smith identifies one as the most prominent: the ability to speak about their faith.

> The vast majority of [American teenagers] were [found] to be *incredibly inarticulate* about their faith, their religious beliefs and practices, and its meaning or place in their lives. We found very few teens from any religious background who are able to articulate well their religious beliefs and explain how those beliefs connect to the rest of their lives.[11]

Though there may be a common bias against teenagers that they are just inarticulate in general, Smith and his colleagues did not find this to be the case. In fact, the teenagers they interviewed were quite articulate regarding a whole range of subjects—from sports to fashion, various school subjects, and even the material they had learned in their sex education classes. In sum, they were articulate about those things for which they were equipped and challenged to become articulate, but their religious beliefs and personal faith were not typically among these items. For the teenagers who were articulate about matters of faith, it was almost invariably the case that their parents were practicing their religion and were themselves articulate about their beliefs.

Coherent and substantive religious identity of parents tends to lead to the coherent and substantive identity of teenagers, while incoherence and insubstantiality also tend to get passed down from one generation to the next. When *The Onion* ran an article with the title "Expectant Parents Throw Some Values Together at Last Minute,"[12] the farcical news source highlighted the very real fact that Smith, Dean, and others have noted: adults—especially parents—effectively form young people according to what and how they themselves believe and what and how they themselves practice. To operate as if a cobbled-together set of vague beliefs would reliably lead to anything other than more of the same is itself farcical. In order, therefore, to make an impact on the quality of belief and religious fluency among young people before they enter into the critical phase of emerging adulthood, the Church must also equip, train, and form adults in the skills and practices that foster confidence in religious particularity and, more specifically, in the understanding of who God is.

In the current setting, the best way to describe the way in which those passing through emerging adulthood understand God is as the "God of the fallback plan" or the "God of the optimistic outlook." In line with what Smith discovered with teenagers, emerging adults tend to foster an implicit belief—one that is sometimes explicitly confessed—that when everything else falls apart or plans do not go as expected, then God will be there to bail you out—like a Cosmic Butler who is at your beck and call. Related to this, God is seen as the guarantor of optimism, the one upon whom many emerging adults project their steady conviction that everything will work out for them in the end, that things always get better, and that every story has a happy ending—that is, like an upbeat therapist.

These vague notions relate to what recent research about those who have left the Church suggests, which is that "former Catholic emerging adults tend to be uncomfortable with firm statements about who or what God is. They like to keep such matters open-ended."[13] On the one hand, emerging adults are hypersensitive to the appearance of intolerance that religious particularity seems to suggest, while on the other hand, notions of God need to remain flexible and amorphous if one is going to be able to fit God into one's own condition as either the last resort or the certifier of better days. What is missing is the challenge, the training, and the tools to change the paradigm from one where preoccupations with remaining inoffensive and unperturbed predominate to one where belief leads to understanding and where religious identity is the foundation for coming to know oneself and the world. In other words, one would begin saying something like, "I am one who is looked upon by the Lord."

In order to gain some perspective on the basic elements of this paradigmatic shift, it is worth quoting Smith and his colleagues at length from the conclusion of their *Young Catholic America*:

> Three major domains appear to influence the religious and spiritual lives of Catholic youth during these years of transition [to emerging adulthood]. The first is *close relationships to religious adults* who help to form youth in their faith, serve as valuable reference points of belief and participation, and make attending Mass more meaningful and rewarding. The second is *internalized religious beliefs and personal religious experiences*, including having a faith that one finds important in daily life, believing in divine miracles, and experiencing answers to prayer. These factors (beliefs and experiences) often play a central role in forming a Catholic worldview and identity, which, once established, are likely to last into emerging adulthood—in part by helping youth understand the deeper, spiritual aspects of their Catholic faith as authentic life truths. And, note, in most cases this second set of factors is modeled and formed (or not) primarily by those involved in the first domain: adults with whom a teen has close and valued relationships. It all ties together. *Religious practices* are the third important component in maintaining Catholic faith and practice during the transition to emerging adulthood. These bolster Catholicism's place as central to a teen's identity and make it a kind of "capital investment" or an accumulating resource with ongoing payoffs, so to speak. Once youth have built up this "religious capital" of know-how in practicing the

faith, they are more likely to take advantage of its rewards by continuing to participate in the Church and believe and live out what it teaches.[14]

Even if there is bad news regarding the religious lives of teen-agers and even worse news about the religious identity of emerging adults as they move toward the more settled identity of adulthood, we would be remiss if we did not also notice the signs of hope contained within this general picture. Even among those young adults who have left the Church, there are stirrings and doubts that are no less significant than the disquietude of those who remain in the Church. From either position, emerging adults reaching the threshold of adulthood are unsettled and questioning. While those of us involved in the religious education and faith formation of the young and not-so-young alike would certainly find inadequate the prevalent notions of God that "former Catholics" foster—as representatives of the wider population—we must also recognize that the remnant of God in their hearts and minds is itself a good thing. The majority of former Catholic young adults are not migrating to atheism but rather something more like apathy or disenchantment.[15] Even a notion of God that begins as a "fallback plan" or "perpetual optimist" may begin to grow toward the unlimited dimensions of the God who creates, sustains, and moves all life in Jesus Christ with the Holy Spirit.

For those emerging adults who are leaving the Church, who have left the Church, or who need further strength to build their life upon the faith of the Church, we might think about our current opportunities for new proclamation of the Gospel in terms of Saint Paul at the Areopagus. Like Paul's interlocutors then, our interlocutors are constantly looking for new things and constantly keeping their options open. If we can appeal to their imaginations and challenge them in the right ways, perhaps they too will say something like those Aeropagites who asked Paul, "May we learn what this new teaching is that you speak of? For you bring some strange notions to our ears; we should like to know what these things mean" (Acts 17:19–20). That is precisely how a liability becomes an asset: when the positive side of deficient notions of God becomes the possibility for wonder and thus transformational growth.

In all this, that statistic with which I started this section about the personal versus impersonal God relative to Catholic versus former Catholic emerging adults stands as a symbol of the entire dynamic. If you never hear your parents tell you they love you, over time you find it difficult to stand upon that belief even if, in truth, your parents do love you. Likewise, if you are not equipped, guided, and even challenged to recognize the personal nature of God and God's investment in everyday life, then over time it becomes more and more difficult to actually believe it. The practice of telling stories of grace is like letting God tell you that you are loved. And as every teacher knows, you truly learn something when you are forced to teach it, which in this case means being "forced" to articulate the story for someone else.

The Mystery of Grace

Describing grace as a disruption of the regular order of things is like describing God as a Divine Butler or Cosmic Therapist. There is a modicum of truth to the description, and yet taking this description as the whole truth parodies grace as those images parody God. What is common to both assumptions is the implicit or even explicit belief that the world is what the world is and that the best we can hope for is maybe some fortuitous interventions to make things in the world turn out better than they would have otherwise. When put in these terms, it is pretty easy to see why the more "sober-minded" among us take religious inclinations as, at best, harmless wishful thinking or, worse, signs of weakness and blindness.

In the next section, I will speak to the importance of story-telling as a way of knowing, but first I want to address this problem of grace. My basic strategy in responding to the outright dismissal or just the prevalent ostracizing and minimizing of grace is not to argue forcefully in response to this charge but instead to recast the understanding of grace entirely. If the popular and broadly operative notion of grace has to do with it being a temporary interruption to what is ordinary, then I intend to flip this notion upside down. In truth, this is not at all my own original idea but rather a recovery of the Catholic understanding of grace itself. In this view, grace pertains much more to what is constant—not variable—while our perceptivity and responsiveness to grace constitute what is subject to change. By this reckoning, when grace interrupts it does so as the seismic shift from a lesser, more limiting order to the grander, more capacious order. Grace is the introduction of what is most original, and it thus redefines what is really "ordinary."

In a short essay titled "Meditation in a Toolshed," C. S. Lewis describes this kind of shift as the difference between looking *at* and looking *along* a beam of light. Lewis invites his readers to imagine themselves standing in a dark toolshed in which there is a single hole in the ceiling through which a beam of light enters. To stand in the darkness and look at the beam of light is one kind of experience, and indeed this experience is about seeing the beam of light as disrupting the ordinary darkness of the toolshed. But if you move underneath the hole in the ceiling and look up along the beam of light, both what you see and how you see shift dramatically. You are still in the same toolshed, and there is still the same beam of light, but you have both changed your position and taken on a new way of seeing. Looking in this way gives you a vision of leaves and trees, and even the sun some ninety million miles away, while allowing you to recognize that the toolshed is situated in a larger world. Even without commenting on the platonic resonances of this image, we can grasp Lewis's point when he pithily states, "Looking along the beam, and looking at the beam are very different experiences."[16] The light is a gift that breaks into what appears ordinary, but does so that you may come to see what is real. The toolshed is not fake, but it does have a context.

To follow Lewis just one step further, we might consider how he constructs the land of Narnia in his beloved *Chronicles*. Children enter into Narnia through some door or other, and both the appearance of the door and the invitation to pass through it are always given as a gift. What happens on the other side of the door is the story of that gift becoming a task, namely, the arduous task of learning how to love Narnia on its own terms. No one is forced to love Narnia; everyone must learn and, in the end, desire to love it. To return to Robert Barron's phrase, becoming the sort of person who is at home in Narnia is very much about taking on a "way of seeing." Learning to see along the "light of Narnia" teaches the children not only how to live *there* but also how to live *here*. Seeing along that light changes not just *what* but also *how* you see.

While systematic exposition is important and necessary for speaking of this shift that grace affects, literary artists—not unlike Caravaggio in his own medium—create narratives and portraits that show us rather than tell us what this paradigmatic shift is like. One particularly compelling example comes from Marilynne Robinson in her novel *Gilead*. While the transformation of vision according to grace is the leitmotif of the entire novel—virtually innumerable specific incidents and elements point to how the whole order of her protagonist's life is shifting toward grace—I simply want to attend to two moments in the novel that, in a way, stand for the whole when they stand together.

In a scene that occurs near the very beginning of the novel, the elderly John Ames—in whose voice the entire novel is written— is recalling an episode from his childhood when he accompanied

his father on a journey from Iowa to Kansas to find the grave
of his paternal grandfather. Having come to the gravesite after
weeks of walking, hunger, and no small amount of hardship, Ames
describes the grave within the ingloriously stark desolation of the
barren plains, where the landscape itself communicates emptiness
and perhaps even sorrow. In this extended passage, though, Ames
recalls how the whole scene shifted for him and, by association,
for his disheartened father:

> Every prayer seemed long to me at that age, and I was truly
> bone tired. I tried to keep my eyes closed, but after a while I
> had to look around a little. And this is something I remem-
> ber very well. At first I thought I saw the sun setting in the
> east; I knew where east was, because the sun was just over
> the horizon when we got there that morning. Then I real-
> ized that what I saw was a full moon rising just as the sun
> was going down. Each of them was standing on its edge,
> with the most wonderful light between them. It seemed as if
> you could touch it, as if there were palpable currents of light
> passing back and forth, or as if there were great taut skeins
> of light suspended between them. I wanted my father to see
> it, but I knew I'd have to startle him out of his prayer, and I
> wanted to do it the best way, so I took his hand and kissed
> it. And then I said, "Look at the moon." And he did. We just
> stood there until the sun was down and the moon was up.
> They seemed to float on the horizon for quite a long time, I
> suppose because they were both so bright you couldn't get a
> clear look at them. And that grave, and my father and I, were
> exactly between them, which seemed amazing to me at the
> time, since I hadn't given much thought to the nature of the
> horizon. My father said, "I would never have thought this
> place could be beautiful. I'm glad to know that."[17]

This peculiarity of light passing between the sun on one
horizon and the moon on the other changed how Ames saw this

otherwise lifeless terrain. Even more, his father, for whom the memory of his own father was riddled with pain and confusion, comes to glimpse, so far as we can tell, how the very landscape that is the symbol of his sorrow and guilt is capable of becoming a place of beauty. At this point in the novel—all of which is told through the elderly Ames's acts of memory—the light that makes things beautiful is something that breaks into the ordinary way of things and changes what is seen for some limited period of time.

By the end of the novel, in what is Ames's final act of memory right before his writing halts as he sleeps into a peaceful death, he returns to what this earlier experience communicated to him. The possibility of a new light breaking into the way things otherwise tend to be and presenting what is "common" or even "painful" as "beautiful" for a period of time was the theme of a Pentecost sermon that he, the long-serving Presbyterian minister, cherished as perhaps the finest and most important work of his preaching ministry. But now, in his most mature reflection, he returns to reflect again upon that sermon and, without casting it aside, wonders if there is something more to say:

> It has seemed to me sometimes as though the Lord breathes on this poor gray ember of Creation and it turns to radiance—for a moment or a year or the span of a life. And then it sinks back into itself again, and to look at it no one would know it had anything to do with fire, or light. That is what I said in the Pentecost sermon. I have reflected on that sermon, and there is some truth in it. But the Lord is more constant and far more extravagant than it seems to imply. Wherever you turn your eyes the world can shine like transfiguration. You don't have to bring a thing to it except a little willingness to see. Only, who could have the courage to see it? . . . Theologians talk about a prevenient grace that precedes grace itself and allows us to accept it. I think there must also be a prevenient courage that allows us to be brave—that is,

to acknowledge that there is more beauty than our eyes can bear.[18]

What this latter passage invites us to consider is how the light of memory changes and even allows the terms of particular events to be recast accordingly. In the first instance, Ames's mature reflection would not have been possible had not something strangely wonderful struck him as a child standing at that gravesite. In what amounted to no more than a flash within the context of a lifetime spanning more than seventy years, the glowing incandescence that seemed to come from elsewhere momentarily transfigured a landscape, an experience, and a set of relationships that, previously and after, were more colorless than not. As a young man, a grown man, and an old man, he held on to that memory. The practice of continually reflecting upon that memory yielded to him, in the end, yet another surprising flash of insight: perhaps what momentarily changed for him as a child was his way of seeing, so that he was able to glimpse, for that delicate moment when the sun and moon gazed at each other, the deeper beauty of a world that is often seen on other terms. In other words, Ames reckons with the possibility that our lives rotate like our planet in relation to the sun: perhaps "light is constant, we just turn over in it. . . . My grandfather's grave turned into the light, and the dew of his weedy little mortality patch was glorious."[19]

Even at the end of a long life, the belief that "the world is charged with the grandeur of God," as Gerard Manley Hopkins put it, is a delicate thing. Part of that belief is recognizing that our own capacity to recognize beauty is itself the variable rather than the constant. The most difficult part of recognizing the beauty that grace reveals is learning what this beauty actually is, because, in the case of the gift of grace, beauty is not always what we expect it to be. God's beauty is so grand that it exceeds and often confounds our own notions of beauty, so that the beauty that the disciple is invited to bear is a beauty that requires the disciple himself to grow, to learn to see anew, and in the end, to expand the possibilities for loving. When Matthew looked back toward Jesus looking upon him, he allowed himself to look along the light of being loved, and that changed him. When Thomas looked upon the wounds of the risen Lord within the gift of peace Jesus offered, his way of seeing shifted. Likewise, for all those—from Pope Francis to John Ames—who struggle and strain to trust themselves to the fundamental belief that "I am one who is looked upon by the Lord," the light of that confession touches everything else.

The problem, of course, is that there are strong competing narratives that teach us to see in other ways and either disorder our view of the world or else make the prospect of building one's life on the disciple's confession a perilous affair. No literary figure in the past hundred years was more attuned to this fact than Flannery O'Connor. On the one hand, O'Connor's presentation of grace could not seem more different from Robinson's, with O'Connor's stories often revolving around violent breaks in the routine order of things, while Robinson concerns herself with the gentle emergence of creation's incandescence. On the other hand, though, both give eloquent witness to the fundamentally transformational quality of grace that will, in decisive moments, appear to disturb what we consider to be the normal order of things, while at other times appearing to perfect that order.

In line with her deeply Thomistic understanding of grace, O'Connor eschews the commonplace understanding of grace as what she dubs "Instant Uplift."[20] This notion of grace keeps grace wholly separate from the operations of the world—with all the world's complexities, ambiguities, and messiness—such that grace breaks in to induce a break out from the confines of the "ordinary." Who wouldn't crave an easy cure to what ails you, such as winning the lottery when you are mired in debt? The problem for O'Connor is that this cheap notion of grace does not take life seriously enough and, moreover, does not correspond to the utter seriousness and oddity of the Incarnation. At the heart of the Christian faith is the mystery of God clinging to this world *in the flesh* in order to redeem and sanctify it rather than replacing it with something else, something "more pleasant." The latter would certainly seem easier, but the beauty of God is that God chooses to enter into our situation. This is the thunderbolt that recurs in O'Connor's literature.

In her stories, grace always arrives as disruption, oftentimes a violent one. The dramatic tension of the narratives, then, corresponds to the arduous task and the demanding journey of envisioning the entire drama in light of the disruption. In this way, the disruption, which begins truly as aberration, becomes the portal of possibility for a whole new order. In one of her most famous stories, "Revelation," the character Ruby Turpin is physically struck between the eyes, and this act of violence ushers in a period of intense disorientation leading, in the end, to a vision of Ruby's own culture turned upside down.[21] If this were Narnia, the sudden, unexpected blow upon her forehead would be the door, and the painful transformation of vision would be learning to negotiate the new terrain on the other side.

In her own setting, O'Connor was reacting to a kind of "do-it-yourself religion" that haunted southern Christians of her era.[22] That description remains apt for us today on an even broader scale. To dictate the terms on which God may be involved in the world—as a fallback plan or guarantor of optimism, a Divine Butler or Cosmic Therapist—is to make God a character in the story we ourselves author. For O'Connor, the first thing grace must do if it is truly grace is to break us from this spell, and just like someone who is deeply asleep, being suddenly awoken has a violent feel. The point of the shock is not, in the end, the shock itself but rather the possibility of beginning to abide according to another narrative, another order. In fact, as O'Connor would contend, this possibility is the beginning of healing us of our intractable dependence upon seeing the world in other terms—ones that insulate us or otherwise remain within the confines of our own preferences.[23] For her as with Robinson and Lewis, grace presents its own terms and provides its own light. The challenge is to learn to see along this light.

This is a way of seeing that takes practice, and learning to see along the beam of grace is, at times, painful. That's because uncertainty is painful, vulnerability is painful, and growth is painful. Grace is serious business because it forces you to take account of both what you see and how you see. If Christian hope concerns the prospect of coming to see all of life and all of creation as created, redeemed, and sanctified in the love of the Father by Jesus Christ in the Holy Spirit, then Christian formation takes the transformation of vision as a fundamental learning objective. Despite what we might otherwise prefer, we do not learn anything instantaneously: not math, not pottery, not love. The same goes for learning to see and trust ourselves to the order of grace, which the flashes of grace announce and which our own responses confirm. In the next chapter, I will present seven principles for learning to observe and then narrate particular experiences of grace, but before I move to that project I want to consider how storytelling is itself a way of knowing and indeed one that is particularly apt for coming to know in the order of grace.

The Practice of Storytelling

Though I previously mentioned the crisis pertaining to emerging adults who are rapidly disengaging from the Church, the project I am proposing is not some kind of emergency effort to save those who are lost. Rather, this is about strengthening everyone: those "within," those at the "door" going in either direction, and those "outside." That's the way communion works, and the Church seeks nothing if not communion.

If we were to look for a point of broad agreement among all emerging adults regardless of religious identity, just as we previously found one that showed the greatest discrepancy between Catholics and former Catholics in this stage (i.e., the belief in a personal God involved in the world), what we would find is that emerging adults are of one mind in regard to the relationship between science and religion—or rather the disjunction between them. In response to the statement that "the teachings of science and religion often ultimately conflict with each other," 59.19 percent of Catholic emerging adults and 59.17 percent of former Catholic emerging adults agreed (plus a fraction more who "strongly agreed"). When the proposal was restated in positive terms—"The findings of science and teachings of religion are entirely compatible with each other"—the responses were consistent: 59.56 percent of Catholic emerging adults disagreed, as did 58.37 percent of former Catholic emerging adults (plus another fraction who "strongly disagreed").[24] On the basis of the interviews that corresponded to these findings, the researchers summarized that the vast majority of emerging adults—again, regardless of religious identity—believes that "science and logic are how we 'really' know things about our world, and religious faith either violates or falls short of the standards of scientific knowledge."[25]

These statistics are emblematic of the general assumption as to the superiority of scientific knowledge. Scientific knowledge is considered mature, sophisticated, and reasonable, while religious knowledge is childish, simple, and even imaginary. In short, the one who knows scientifically is serious, and the one who knows religiously is lax. In all of this it is clear that by broad cultural consensus we assent to a claim about what kinds of things are knowable or even desirable for knowledge as well as to what ways of knowing are legitimate. Along with these agreements as to the objects of knowledge and ways of knowing, we also happen to make a claim about who we are as the ones who know or can know. If empirical data determine the range of knowledge and only the ways of knowing that correspond to these data are deemed fully valid, then we thereby declare ourselves to be consumers of data who acquire and test data in, ideally, completely objective and disinterested ways. We tend to conceive of ourselves only as creatures who engage in the pursuits of instrumental reason because we tend to deem useful only what serves the purposes we ourselves have approved of, whether in the name of progress, advancement, or "science."[26]

Blessed John Henry Newman critiques this delimitation of objects of knowledge, ways of knowing, and thus the reduction of us human beings as only "rational knowers" over and over again throughout his preaching and writing. In one of his most sophisticated works, he very plainly claims what our actions show to be true: "After all, man is *not* a reasoning animal; he is a seeing, feeling, contemplating, acting animal. . . . Life is for action. If we insist on proofs for every thing, we shall never come to action: to act you must assume, and that assumption is faith."[27] Newman thought of himself and each of us as "whole persons" who are never reducible to one dimension or another, and this includes our intellect, our faculties for reasoning. That Newman himself defends this view is no small matter since few match his own intellectual prowess. When he speaks of himself and his own journey toward a deeper understanding of the reality of things that he identifies with a way of knowing by faith, he recognizes that scientific reasoning cannot, by itself, account for what it means to "know" and "act" as a whole human being. "For myself," Newman writes, "it was not logic that carried me on; as well might one say that the quicksilver in the barometer changes the weather. It is the concrete being that reasons; pass a number of years, and I find my mind in a new place; how? the whole man moves; paper logic is but the record of it."[28]

The demanding question that follows from Newman's thought for educators like myself is, "Do we educate the whole person?" If in our schools, parishes, and families we value scientific reasoning as the most important or, in the extreme, the only measure of growing in knowledge and in the ability to make judgments, then those we form will grow according to what we have valued for them. "It is very well," Newman argues, "to freshen our impressions and convictions from physics, but to create [our convictions] we must go elsewhere."[29] Intellectual growth that includes developing the capacity for scientific reasoning must be accompanied by moral education, emotional education, and indeed religious education. This is precisely what is missing in the modern world, and young people are not sufficiently formed or educated as whole persons. As we argued earlier, what happens in childhood and adolescence impacts the state of emerging adults and, subsequently, mature adults. The irony is that even children, but especially teenagers, *naturally* and dare I say *instinctively* desire a comprehensive view of things, and they react as if to an allergen when they think they are only getting part of the picture from others, especially from adults. Why is it that a young person is so sensitive to inauthenticity? Because she seeks the whole and hates when she doesn't get it.

In addition to treating human beings as whole persons who are created to learn, know, and act accordingly, Newman also places great emphasis on the importance of the "concrete" over the "abstract." Pope Francis follows Newman's prioritization on this point when he repeatedly privileges the "concrete Catholic thing"—meaning practices, rituals, and encounters—over what he chides as "airspray" ideas or ideals.[30] Like Flannery O'Connor's understanding of grace, the priority of the concrete respects the decisive difference the Incarnation makes. In this regard, the incarnational impulse of Christianity in general and Catholicism in particular reveals the truth that human nature is "more affected by the concrete than by the abstract."[31] The test of any theory is its suitability for accurately describing and humanly shaping life, just as doctrine draws its meaning from the life of Christ and shapes the lives of Christians in communion. In terms of both the holistic nature of knowledge and the priority of the concrete over the abstract, all knowing is fundamentally about acts of communication. As "knowers," we do not merely learn data objectively and pass on data disinterestedly; rather, we engage in giving and receiving ourselves in what we learn and pass on. To treat the world or our own existence as only a subject to be studied and to learn *about* is to reduce ourselves to processing machines. The whole point of Christian existence is to "live and move and have our being" in Christ (Acts 17:28), that is, to "know" *this* concrete person as the one who embraces our whole being. This is the strongest and most substantial goal for identity formation.

Teenagers and emerging adults are not primarily to blame for the distrust of religious knowledge, especially when juxtaposed with scientific knowledge. In point of fact, we demand much, much more culturally and educationally from each other in terms of what and how we strive to learn in the mode of scientific inquiry than we do in the mode of religious inquiry. We seek precision with science; we move from theory to experiment, verification, and reporting; and we pass on ideals that uphold the value of this level of accountability. All too often with religious knowledge, we seek not to judge, not to demand too much, and not to question our own or others' experiences, and we allow for vague statements and imprecise accounts to go virtually unchecked. Moreover, we pass on a value of accountability here too, but it is of remarkably low value. We ask too little of those we educate and form—and, quite frankly, of ourselves—when it comes to religious knowledge. Abstractions, vagaries, platitudes, and generalities pass as satisfactory in this realm, but we would never allow those to pass where scientific knowledge is concerned. Why do we require less of those things that involve the "whole person" than we do of those things that involve the brain alone? In matters concerning the whole person, we must step in rather than st---d---t

disinterestedly, all while paying as close attention to experiences—
especially those that shock, trouble, and enlighten us—as we would
if we were observing chemicals in a laboratory. The science of grace is
every bit as demanding—if not more demanding—than the hardest
of hard sciences. Just like any science, it begins with keen observations and rapt attentiveness, like an adolescent noticing the effect
of the light passing between the sun and the moon on an otherwise
desolate Kansan plain.

Grace demands that we pay attention and learn to speak in
specific terms, as does the practice of storytelling. When someone is
forced to speak in specific terms about the concrete realities of life,
the abstract theories breakdown; they are shown to be inauthentic
under the weight of reality, just as scientific experimentation and
reporting disprove inadequate hypotheses. Just so, the challenge
of crafting a story forces the storyteller to move from abstractions
(for example, "love is kind" or "friendship means always being
ready to forgive") to a lived, personal reality. This is not at all to
suggest that everyone will have his or her own individual reality,
as if this were merely a retreat into private experience, but rather
to suggest that the project of telling a story about real-life events
and encounters provides a prime opportunity for recognizing the
insufficiency of broad notions and platitudes for describing and
shaping the concreteness of human life. Moreover, the whole point
of storytelling is to communicate this experience, event, or encounter to someone else. *don't give ppl generalizations,*
give them your experiences so they can create

The complexities and grit of being "kind in love," for example, cannot be observed in maxims but only in the particularities
of embodied experience. Parents know this because the kindness
of love moves from ideal notion to concrete thing in the course
of cleaning up the twelfth cup of milk your three-year-old spilled
this week and learning not to begrudge but somehow love him
more because of it, even while also growing in annoyance. The

necessity of forgiveness in friendship passes from idea to reality when the friend with whom you make yourself most vulnerable uses something you shared in confidence to gain esteem for herself in the eyes of others, to get ahead for an honor, or merely to push you down a little bit out of envy. The messiness of that project of forgiveness and then the reconciliation to follow is too untidy for bumper-sticker spiritualities. The wildness of forgiveness is even more ferociously pressed upon you when you are the one in need of being forgiven. In instances such as these, if you want to recognize the humanity of all these actions, you must "force" yourself to tell the story of what happened and what it means.

The most important matters of being human cannot be reduced to empirical observations, abstract theories, or parcels of data, even though these matters do not invalidate what we can know "scientifically." Furthermore, the skills of paying close attention to the facts that are cultivated through both liberal arts and scientific education alike enable one to become a more practiced observer of concrete realities. Even as you begin with paying attention, the qu"estion each of us faces over and over again throughout our lives—"Who are you?"—breaks through whenever you must make a determination about the sort of person you are and the kind of world you think we live in. Do we live in a world that, at best, has fleeting moments of beauty, or do we live in a world where beauty abounds but our receptiveness and responsiveness to this deep beauty varies? Are we observers and data processors, or are we lovers and free persons who communicate ourselves to one another? When we make claims about the approved or legitimate ways of knowing, we are also making claims about the meaning of the world, the prospect of human dignity, and the status of beauty.

You cannot explain love by the laws of physics, and you cannot explain forgiveness with psychoanalytic theory. To give an adequate account of human life requires the full measure of being human, with all its ways of knowing. In regard to storytelling, only rich stories do justice to rich experiences. Grace observes, confirms, and elevates the complexities of human nature, and "grace is not so poor a thing that it can't present itself in any number of ways."[32] When parents learn the depths of loving their child, they contemplate a deeper order to the world and come to redefine what is "ordinary." When you forgive or are forgiven by your friend, you assent to the possibility of forgiveness that neither of you invented but that you discovered only through participation. Learning what that forgiveness means and what it signifies requires unfailing attentiveness to the particularities of your situation and the complexities of the friendship and the circumstances alike. If these are occasions of grace, then they demand clinging to the wholeness of what it means to be human, and inversely, if you seek to deal with the whole of what it means to be human, then you are already searching for grace.

We learn through communication. Even beyond the "softest" of all sciences—that pertaining to human relationships and emotions—this is the basic fact in *every* process of coming to know, including the "hard sciences." Despite what we moderns tend to think about the transfer of information in what we consider the most legitimated ways of knowing—as if parcels of knowledge pass into and out of us like memory sticks in a USB drive—we always share some of ourselves in every act of communication, both in giving and in receiving. Storytelling blatantly acknowledges this fact.

Francesca Murphy describes well this phenomenon of "personal" communication and the way in which we tend to leave the personal dimension unaccounted for when she writes that "dialogue partners communicate something of themselves, and it is this *act* of putting oneself across which never quite figures in the reconfiguration of meaning."[33] Even more, the quality of a story always correlates to the concreteness of its images and its narrative elements. The more concrete something is, the more difficult it is to generalize. If you craft and tell the story of what you experienced, encountered, or discovered, you also at the same time identify yourself as the one affected. We forget factoids all the time, but stories stay with us. Herein lies some of the antidote to the abstracting and vaporizing tendencies of contemporary spirituality, where God is ambiguous and so then is grace. If any one of us sat in Matthew's place, what would be more eloquent, more beautiful, more observant, and more accurate than telling someone else the story about how "I am the one whom the Lord looked upon"?

Transformation of Vision

Grace deals with the revolution of the ordinary, and storytelling concerns the whole person moving from the abstract to the concrete. In response to both the crisis and the opportunity of identity exploration that occurs especially in emerging adulthood but touches all other stages of life, the embrace of the mystery of grace through the practice of storytelling promises a challenging, rewarding, and very real way to renew and strengthen the efforts of the new evangelization for those in, leaving, or even currently "out" of the Church—at whatever distance from the life of faith. In the chapters to follow, I will first offer seven principles for crafting and sharing stories of grace; then I will analyze selections of stories of grace from emerging adults and adults in order to highlight the concreteness of the beauty they perceive; finally, I will offer suggestions for how this practice may be incorporated into parish, school, and family settings.

As a conclusion to this chapter, I would like to offer a reflection in three parts as to how crafting and sharing stories of grace serve the transformation of disciples' visions of themselves in learning, over and over again, how to see themselves in the light of the Lord's merciful gaze. This transformation in seeing both emerges from and contributes to the core of the disciples' identity. The three parts of this final reflection acknowledge three of the distinctive spectral colors that burst forth from the glorious light of grace.

Full of Grace

Can an experience, a story, or a person ever be *full* of grace? If grace were truly full, wouldn't the everydayness of the experience, the details of the story, or the humanity of the person be overtaken by divine presence? It might seem so. And yet, the one whom we acclaim to be *full of grace*—Mary, Mother of God—is also the one whom Catholics celebrate as the most perfect creation and thus most fully capable of exercising her will in favor of God's Word. With her, to be *full of grace* is, paradoxically, also to be a human being fully alive. Humanity, as it turns out, grows in direct rather than converse proportion to its openness to the divine.[34] When we likewise allow the movements of the Spirit to interpret both who we are and the stories of our lives, then we too begin to fill with grace. To be open to grace and to respond to it changes who we are. The one who grows in response to grace becomes one who is shaped in and by grace—that is, *graceful*.

Full of Wonder

How often do we allow ourselves to truly, deeply wonder? It seems that the common modern practice is to analyze, explain, and categorize phenomena to account for them according to predetermined standards of interpretation. We tend to fit new experiences into fixed worldviews—like new wine in an old wineskin (see Mk 2:22)—or otherwise disregard them. Yet all true learning, growth, and even conversion begins with an openness to wonder. If nothing else, wonder is the implicit admission that what confronts us is something unique, something new, and perhaps something that will stir, challenge, or even revolutionize what we previously assumed. The one

wonder → humility → assurance

who wonders is thus humble, and humility is the necessary posture for faith. "Faith," we are told, "is the assurance of things hoped for, the conviction of things not seen" (Heb 11:1, RSV). With the eyes of faith, we perceive the imperceptible, we approach the ungraspable, and we assent to the irreducible. In an act of trust, faith places us outside our closed worldviews and leads us into a denser and more glorious reality that both supports and transcends yet nevertheless penetrates everyday life. Perhaps one will continue to grow in humility and faith so that the basic orientation of life is one of wonder, maybe even gratitude, for that which cannot be reduced to something lesser. In this way, the one who wonders may just become *wonderful*.

Make Believe

Many would consider the imagination to be the faculty that allows us to escape from reality and to fantasize, that is, to *make believe*. Many filmmakers, novelists, and other artists exercise their some-times-considerable talent in creating alternate realities that will not come to pass. They thus seem to have the most active and acute imaginations among us. But did J. R. R. Tolkien tell stories about Middle Earth as an alternate reality, or did he say things *there* that are deeply true *here and now* but could not be said or heard according to the way we speak in the here and now? When C. S. Lewis imagined a land called Narnia, was he creating a world to which children could escape, or was he hoping to teach them (along with big, dull children like ourselves) how to live fully in this world? Might it be possible that imagination has everything to do with how we are to live in the everyday? Maybe imagination loosens the grip of "rampant secularism," "saturated sensitivities," "the technological meta-culture," and "the dictatorship of relativism."[35] Imagination is about seeing, and both what we see and how we see impacts who we are and who we become. Images make impressions upon our minds

and hearts, they evoke responses, and they speak to us. While most
will probably always associate imagination with *make believe*, we
might recognize movement along another valence: the imagination
allows our *belief to make us*.

Chapter 2

Bending Light

Responding to God's Humility with Disciplined Creativity

God is the extravagant giver of gifts: God both speaks to us in his Word and gives us the freedom to hear and respond. The meaning of discipleship abides in this mystery of hearing and responding (see Lk 8:21, 11:28; cf. Jn 15:14). When C. S. Lewis presents Aslan singing all creation into being in *The Magician's Nephew,* he is transposing the biblical authors' testimony about the Father speaking his Word, Jesus Christ, as the source of all life.[1] To grow as disciples is to learn to live in the Spirit of God's Word, to become ever more mature, capable, and creative dialogue partners in faith.[2] Since God speaks first—God always makes the first move—the freedom of our response depends on first receiving well. Like any good conversation, listening well enables generous, appropriate, and relevant speaking. In the dialogue of faith, each of us must first listen to God's Word, while those of us called to teach others how to speak in this dialogue must therefore teach them how to listen attentively or, to switch metaphors, to see clearly. Seeking to enable others to speak for themselves is very different from expecting them to speak *by* themselves.

The problem with an approach to telling stories of grace that leaves young people, emerging adults, or any of us with minimal guidance is that the stories may often end up only vaguely resembling the Christian faith.[3] Such stories are typically more about "making sense for oneself" than responding to God's address. Clichés, generally accepted principles, and premature explanations can cover up the specific points where the thick reality of grace is present: the precise ways in which God has spoken and is speaking the Word who is Christ. "Everything happens for a reason" becomes the easy answer to disappointment and failure. "God just wanted her in heaven" is cheap balm in the face of death. "I just need to let go and let God" turns a potentially meaningful insight into an act of separation between one's own efforts and the action of grace. Without being challenged and guided, most young people (and adults for that matter) will land on one or another of these ways of expressing their experience of grace, because learning to speak of grace *as grace* is hard work.

Grace is irreducible, incomparable, and altogether peculiar. Flannery O'Connor, who wanted nothing less than to speak of grace *as it is*, said that if you remove the strangeness of grace from a Christian story, then what you are left with is not worth anyone's attention. By reflex, we usually want to look away from grace or else look at grace in a comfortable way, but grace remains unseen unless it is seen on its own terms, as the inbreaking of God's light that reveals Christ's life given for the world. This is a blinding light in which one must learn to see or, rather, *by which* one must learn to see (see Ps 36:10). "Our age . . . does not have a very sharp eye for the almost imperceptible intrusions of grace,"[4] O'Connor declared, and so the "sharpening of the eye" is a goal for those of us who form others in faith, capacitating them to see in light of the mystery of grace in the world. Noting the oddity of grace amid what seem to be the commonplace conditions of the world is the first step in coming to see all things in the order of grace.

If we simply settle for disciples telling their own stories with an emphasis on the uniqueness of their style but not the character of their content, then a peculiarly modern axiom has been assumed: all perspectives are equally valid so long as one claims a perspective as one's own.[5] Faith thus becomes an issue of the strength of one's commitment without accounting for that to which one makes a commitment. With an imbalanced emphasis on individual expression, a theological educator or pastoral minister might come to confirm just about any story regarding faith that a young person tells so long as that young person has claimed the story as his or her own. Stories conforming to this expectation are often deemed unimpeachable because, it is assumed, no one has the right to question another person's "experience." By extension, then, no one has the right to question another person's articulation of faith. Our approach to helping disciples enter into the dialogue of faith is different because the content of the faith matters. I propose starting not with "experience" but with Christ: the love of God whom the Spirit pours into our hearts (see Rom 5:5). He reveals the meaning of our experience to us: God speaks first so that we speak aright when we learn how to listen and respond to his Word (see Ps 51:17).

All the same, the focus on content brings its own dangerous temptation. This is a temptation that most if not all theological educators and pastoral ministers—along with parents—have faced at one time or another: the urge to control. Sometimes this urge is made manifest in a desire for doctrinal inerrancy, by which demands are placed upon growing disciples to speak with unfailing theological precision at all times. By gently critiquing this understandable desire that arises from a commitment to the objective truth of the faith, I am not retreating to the position critiqued earlier where the concern for the content of the faith functionally disappears from view. What I am suggesting is that it is unrealistic to expect those who are learning the language of faith to speak with perfect fluency while engaged in one of the very exercises by which they are developing fluency. All worthwhile intermediate language classes operate with the same set of expectations, as do classes in engineering, philosophy, painting, and vocal performance at a similar level. Expertise is acquired with practice; it is not given in advance. While this practice must certainly be disciplined, it cannot become overly formulaic, for then the personality of the storyteller is drained out of the process. Oftentimes, an exaggerated concern for the proper formula for a story of grace leads to something like a "Mad-Libs" template where the craft of storytelling is reduced to inserting various details into the blank spaces of a preordained framework. This would be like concerning ourselves only with the transmission of data rather than with personal communication. Style matters because the personhood of the speaker matters.

The approach I am recommending holds content, style, discipline, and creativity in tension. It matters that disciples learn to speak rightly according to the content of the faith, *and* it matters that they speak as themselves, with personality.[6] In order to attend to both sides of this tension, those of us who cultivate disciples for the dialogue of faith must concern ourselves not just with the stories that are told but also and especially with the persons who are telling them. In other words, the goal of enabling disciples to tell stories of grace depends upon and does not in any way replace the responsibilities for good faith formation.

What I offer in this chapter thus assumes elements of such formation: catechetical instruction, liturgical participation and training, practicing the works of mercy, establishing mentoring relationships, and immersion within the Christian community, to name a few. I offer seven principles for enabling anyone—youth, emerging adults, and mature adults—to craft meaningful stories of grace that combine the articulation of faith with the expression of identity. These are guiding principles more than steps in a "how-to" list because trying to turn Christian storytelling into some kind of technology is self-defeating: freedom and creativity are squashed in the process. Developing these seven principles will take up most of the rest of this chapter, but first I offer an unusual example of teaching novices how to understand and speak a new kind of story that will help us understand our own task a little better.

Communicating from 250,000 Miles Away

Neil Armstrong was the first human being to see the moon from its surface, but Dave Scott saw it better. In 1971, after already successfully landing on the moon thrice with one "successful failure" mixed in (Apollo 13), NASA was intent to scientifically study the lunar surface. In order to do so, NASA needed geologists to critically evaluate the moon to determine what rocks were worth studying and in which way. The problem, of course, was that the NASA astronauts were not geologists. NASA thus had three options: try to program robots to do the work of geologists on the moon, try to prepare geologists for space travel, or try to make astronauts into geologists. NASA went with the third option, preferring it to the first because of the nonsubstitutability of real-time human judgments and preferring it to the second because, well, they couldn't quite imagine the ordinary scientists they knew surviving this kind of space travel. And so the success of Apollo 15 depended upon NASA's ability to teach Commander Dave Scott and his crew how to see the moon *as geologists*.

The tenth episode of HBO's miniseries *From the Earth to the Moon* tells the story of these Apollo 15 astronauts.[7] The majority of this episode follows the intensive education the astronauts received for doing field geology (lunar field geology!) under the direction of Professor Lee Silver of the California Institute of Technology. After a good deal of time in the classroom and reading textbooks, Professor Silver takes his class of four astronauts out into the field to show them what their education is really all about. The initial vantage point for learning this lesson is a peak overlooking the rugged California desert.

From high above the rocky desert, Professor Silver looks out upon the majestic terrain that excites and energizes him: "This is

Disneyland for us field geologists." His pupils are unimpressed: to them, this is a hot and dusty waste of time. The point of standing high above the variegated terrain below is to get a sense for the "context" of where they are and what they will later learn to see. This is the first step of Silver's incredibly difficult task: to get these seemingly unwilling students to wonder at and enjoy what he himself wonders at and enjoys as a field geologist. This transformation begins with a single rock.

Professor Silver points to this small rock and asks one of the astronauts to pick it up and to tell him about it. "Just start with what you see," Silver says. The astronaut knows enough to recognize the rock as "granite, which is an igneous rock." "Good," Silver responds, "but how did it get here? I don't see any granite here." And speaking to the rock, he asks, "How did you get here, my little friend?" The answer, he indicates, rests in the geological field below. So he leads his mildly bemused but mostly annoyed astronaut pupils into the ravines of the California desert.

With walls of rock reaching high above the students as they walk in the middle of the terrain they first overlooked, Silver announces that there is a story surrounding them, a story of battles won and lost, of peaceful times, and of great upheaval that has played out over the millennia. "Something happened here, something big." In these silent and still walls of striped and peculiarly shaped rocks, including that one particular piece of granite with which they started, is a story—a bevy of stories even—just waiting to be told. "Do you see it yet? It's all pretty much here, in a language you can't yet understand. But it's here."

As this scene unfolds, at least two things are happening. First, Professor Silver is proposing something. He is proposing that there is meaning where none is immediately apparent. He is proposing that this meaning is not just a matter of what is there but also (even more crucially) a matter of how to interpret what is there. He is proposing that it matters very much that they pay close attention to what is around them—"just start with what you see"—and that it matters very much that they learn what it means to really see it.

Second, and just as important, Professor Silver is beginning to appeal to the imaginations of his pupils. It would not be enough for him to desire for them to see; they have to desire it for themselves. They've already studied a sufficient amount to learn the basics of geology; they are able to employ certain terminology and to begin to make certain kinds of distinctions. Now he needs them to become curious enough to want to understand particular things in their context. To see the particular things—such as a single granite rock—and their context together will enable them to better determine which items to pick up and question in the first place. In order to see the story he is asking them to see and indeed to tell, the astronauts must both investigate the particular things well and wonder about these particular things in the context of their surroundings and as part of a larger meaning. "That's what we field geologists are: storytellers . . . interpreters, actually."

This is the whole point of their education: *they* have to learn to see so *they* can tell the story of what they discover. From 250,000 miles away, they will be the ones to decide what is important to study, to question what they see, and to make decisions about what to bring back to Earth for further analysis. The final goal of this education is not for them to be able to understand what Professor Silver says and listen to him tell the story; in the end, they are the ones who must tell the story to those who are not in a position to see what they will see.

In the concluding scene of the episode, this is precisely what happens. Dave Scott picks up what NASA later dubbed a "genesis rock," which was formed more than four billion years ago, shortly after our solar system itself was formed. To the untrained and uninterested eye, this rock would probably not have drawn much attention. For Dave Scott, though, who had been trained and who had learned to want to see the moon with both acuity and wonder, this rock promised a fantastic story.

I have chosen to spend some time with this episode of *From the Earth to the Moon* because much of what this show portrays relates to what I will share later. In the coming pages, I will emphasize the importance of starting with what you see, learning to see and speak in a certain way, and communicating well so that others may understand what they do not see themselves. I invite you to keep this somewhat unusual example in mind not quite as a strict allegory but rather as a kind of model of what we are hoping to prepare storytellers to do and to become.

Seven Principles for Finding, Crafting, and Sharing Stories of Grace

Since its inception in the summer of 2002, Notre Dame Vision (which I direct) has featured stories of grace as part of its teaching curriculum. We sensed from the beginning that these stories were somehow a necessary ingredient to hosting a faith-formation retreat experience for teenagers, even if we didn't fully grasp why they were necessary. Initially, those of us on the leadership team did not do all that much to guide our college students as they crafted these stories: we had so many of these college students every year (upward of seventy) and needed only so many stories for the summer program (fifteen or so) that we always seemed to get enough quality stories to fill our schedule.

After a few years, though, we started to work more directly and intentionally with those whom we selected to offer stories in the summer. We started by engaging in a collaborative editing process with the college students as we assisted them in refining their stories and especially shaping them for the particular teenage audiences with whom they would share them. Through editing and finishing this work, we started to notice certain trends in how the college mentors articulated their faith in and through these stories. For example, while they genuinely believed in something like grace operating in and through their life experiences, they were generally imprecise or uncertain in their manner of speaking about grace. At critical moments in a story, clichés and colloquialisms tended to keep these experiences from feeling as real or personal to the audience as they might have otherwise been; even more, the storytellers themselves were often frustrated because they sensed there was more to what they were trying to say than what they were actually able to articulate.

The college mentors also dealt with a creeping concern about the emotional appeal of their stories. They'd wonder if their stories were deep enough, big enough, and significant enough. They'd struggle with comparing their stories to their peers' in terms of how strongly the stories tugged on the heartstrings of listeners. In short, even though we were "getting what *we* needed" to fill out our retreat schedule, we still had a lot of work to do to guide our student ministers in articulating and sharing their faith through stories, to help them grow as disciples through the practice of storytelling. Since we were asking these college students to be models and indeed guides for the high school participants as they worked on articulating their own faith, our responsibility for better preparing our seventy college students annually was proving more and more important.

We decided, therefore, that alongside the ongoing development of a special theology course designed for our mentors—through which we cultivated their theological imaginations—we would also provide ample structure and support to our college mentors as they crafted "witness talks" (stories of grace) that were the capstone projects for the pastoral skills workshop we offered them during the spring semester. Instead of only working closely with the fifteen or so mentors whose stories we selected for sharing at our summer program, we began working with all of them to develop them as

Christian storytellers who would become more and more capable of speaking compellingly about their experiences of grace, who could express themselves more genuinely than clichés and colloquialisms would allow, and who were able to offer others trustworthy examples of what prayerful, patient, theologically informed reflections of faith are like. When they shared these stories, they were also sharing themselves as ones who had come to see in the light of God's mercy.

As fruit of more than a decade of working with these college students, we established these seven basic principles to guide them in finding, crafting, and sharing stories of grace:

1.   Tell it as a story.

2.   Begin with what happened.

3.   Express it in style.

4.   Modify it for your audience.

5.   Ensure there is sufficient closure.

6.   Embrace natural emotions.

7.   Pray and practice.

It bears repeating that these guiding principles do not comprise a recipe; rather, they help our youth and young adults—as well as those of us responsible for their formation—pursue the deeper potential and meaning that the art of crafting stories of grace promises.

1. Tell It as a Story

It seems obvious, but it is incredibly important and easy to forget when setting out to tell a story of grace that the task at hand is to tell a *story*. The task is *not* to write a homily, teach a lesson, make an argument, or simply recount the facts of an event. This is not about preaching, debating, or reporting; it's about telling a story. If lessons, messages, and reminders come through in the process, they will come through in the course of the story. Remembering the priority of storytelling both limits the scope of what one is expected to do and frees one to do this one thing well.

Like the seventh principle that we will explore below ("pray and practice"), this first principle pertains to the entire process rather than one moment in the process. Making the task clear for the one who is charged with crafting and sharing a story of grace allows him or her to begin with some sense of what the end of the creative process will yield. For example, with our college mentors for Notre Dame Vision, they know up front that their objectives are to create five- to seven-minute oral stories for a high-school audience. For the mentors, this idea of presenting to a live audience in a limited amount of time informs their work of discovering a story worth telling, shaping it for this specific purpose, and refining it for a particular audience in an oral form.

To give another example, in a theology course I teach called "The Character Project: Grace and Becoming Fully Human," I give my students an assignment that requires them to both orally share one of these five- to seven-minute stories with their classmates and submit a written (academically) annotated version of their stories to me.[8] In addition to thinking about sharing their stories orally with their classmates, as they go along in the creative process they must also take note of how what we studied over the course of the semester illuminates aspects of their stories, helps them to recognize the various dimensions of their stories, and provides them with language and categories for analyzing and understanding their own life experiences more richly. In making clear what I expect them to create, I thus help them distinguish this assignment in terms of purpose, method, and responsibilities from the various other written assignments they complete throughout the semester. It is my responsibility to present them with the task of telling a story and, moreover, to describe for them what kind of story I am inviting them to craft and, in two different ways, deliver.

Of course, the first step in telling a story is finding a story worth telling.[9] For would-be storytellers, it is always tempting to begin by considering the point they want to make or the impression they want to give. This is a temptation very much worth resisting. For those of us who design retreats, we may take a certain comfort in establishing the topics or themes for retreat talks first, then assigning these themes or topics to specific persons, and then asking those persons to craft stories that are made to fit. While recognizing that this is oftentimes the most practical way to complete a schedule, I advise against this approach. By this method, the would-be storytellers are expected to read one of their own life stories in a predetermined way, one that threatens to dull the particularity and peculiarity of a revelation of grace from the outset. At Notre Dame Vision, we do have specific thematic areas for the "witness talks" that are ultimately shared during our summer program, but we tell our mentors who are crafting stories to let us worry about the category. We present them with guiding questions to aid them in their reflection, but we ultimately give them freedom to explore the potential stories from their lives. For our part, rather than leading our students to ask, "What story can I find to fit this spot?" we want our students to ask, "What story do I have to share? What potential story is worth exploring? What should I wonder about and ponder from my own life?"

To prepare someone to "tell a story," it is critical for that person to see, as well as he or she can, what actually happened. In short, what are the facts? What's really there? What is there to see? Jumping too quickly or too soon to an interpretation of the meaning of what happened runs the risk of turning a potential story of grace into a generic homily or platitude. If the experience pertains to the divorce of parents, then the particular moments, people, feelings, confusions, and oddities of that predictably messy time must be claimed, recorded, and eventually pondered and prayed over. If the experience concerns forgiveness and reconciliation, the nature of the offense and the nature of the healing are both important, for grace never erases but always transforms the "stuff" of real, human life. This truth relates to any and every experience that is a candidate for yielding a story of grace. Every good story begins with the willingness and patience to *see* well—that is, to genuinely receive—in, along with, amidst, and through the messiness and inerasable thickness of particular human lives and relationships. Paying close attention and seeking to perceive before judging or interpreting is the first step to telling a good story.

2. Begin with What Happened

If the objective is to tell a story of grace that duly respects historical particularity, then we should place the initial emphasis upon what happened. Consider, for example, the healing of the blind man in the ninth chapter of John's gospel. In the course of the larger story recorded in the chapter, the man healed of blindness tells the basic story of what happened to him three times. When he is first questioned about what happened to him, he recounts his story in literal detail: "The man called Jesus made clay and anointed my eyes and told me, 'Go to Siloam and wash.' So I went there and washed and was able to see" (Jn 9:11). When asked a second time, this time by the Pharisees, he repeats the core of his story: "He put clay on my eyes, and I washed, and now I can see" (9:15b). After the Pharisees question his parents and then return to ask the man again what happened to him, "he answered, 'If [Jesus] is a sinner, I do not know. One thing I do know is that I was blind and now I see'" (9:25). Only after this man thrice recalls what happened to him does the evangelist make the connection between the physical act of seeing and the spiritual seeing that comes by way of an act of faith. This once blind man waits upon the full meaning of what has happened to him—he does not presume meaning too quickly. He doesn't presume to know why this happened to him, nor does he really understand how. He simply begins with what happened to him, and he implicitly claims this as something worthy of wonder.

For the once-blind man, the movement from physical seeing to deeper spiritual seeing comes in response to Jesus' well-placed question: "When Jesus heard that they had thrown him out, he found him and said, 'Do you believe in the Son of Man?'" (Jn 9:35). The healed man's experience is most emphatically *not* one of self-discovery; rather, his experience of grace is relational and indeed dialogical. He is given the right question at the right time, then he is given the information and means necessary to formulate a response (see 9:36–38), and only thus does the gospel writer bring the story of this man to a close: "He said, 'I do believe, Lord'; and he worshiped him" (9:38).

The event of this man's physical healing was like that single piece of granite in the astronaut's hand in the middle of the California desert: by starting with what was actually there, the right sort of questions began to arise—why? how?—that eventually led to the deeper significance of the story. If that man from John 9 were to tell his story later—as he surely must have—he would certainly have recounted what physically happened to him in order to give a full and adequate account of the spiritual seeing into which Jesus invited him. His larger story will entail his assent to the *meaning* of what happened, but this statement of meaning depends upon rather than negates or blurs the historical events. Starting with what one sees—in a literal sense—is a necessary basis for both finding and beginning to craft a story. Historical particularity guards against both fantasy and mythology as grace deals with the particularly historical creation that the Word of God assumed in the Incarnation. Responding to that Word with a story of grace is a response in kind.

So what happened? While others may be able to suggest possible story candidates, the storytellers themselves have privileged access to their life experiences. Furthermore, once a potential story is identified, storytellers more than anyone else are capable of and responsible for bringing forth the content of the stories. The more that is brought forth, the more there is for a mentor to work with when guiding the storyteller. We might think of this as establishing the terrain through which the minister or educator can lead the student toward a new way of seeing, similar to how Professor Silver led his astronauts through the ravines of the California desert. This pattern of discovery points to the truth that no one is able to see everything in his or her own life or see the full meaning of anything independent of assistance, and in addition to those astronauts we might also think again of the depths of "seeing" to which Jesus eventually led the man he healed of blindness. In any event, it is nevertheless true that stories of grace cannot emerge without the storytellers themselves taking a primary role in "seeing," in terms of both bringing forth the "stuff of life" and learning how to "see anew." Since grace conforms to and transforms the particularities of our lives, the particularities of experiences and relationships are important.

Something as ordinary as journaling is a helpful aid in drawing out the emerging stories. Even on the most factual level, by simply recalling events and feelings, the details of settings, conversations, and people brings forth important material for the eventual crafting of a story. The content of stories in large part depends on this "stuff."

3. Express It in Style

Stories are much more than just facts: they are acts of communication that include form, intentional shaping, and distinctive modes of expression. We know a story when we hear one. Style matters for telling a story. At the same time, we also know what it's like to encounter something that is more form than substance, where style overwhelms content. Whereas our first two principles relate to establishing the genre as well as the priority of content, this third principle concerns the proper and ordered integration of content with style.

True art is extraordinary creativity within extraordinary discipline. Artists inherit and depend upon much that they do not themselves create. Their creation begins with learning how to receive well, how to see well, and how to be attentive to the "stuff" itself. What we established above holds true: recognizing "what happened" or "what is happening" is the beginning of good storytelling, which will then continue with the creative shaping of a story. In a voice full of honesty, Flannery O'Connor confessed to the challenge people of faith face when they seek to tell a story. For an artist such as herself, it would seem as if faith dispenses her from the responsibility to see clearly; conversely, she argues, faith requires artists to see even more clearly if their art is to be truly sacramental, that is, concerned with what is real:

> Students often have the idea that the process at work [in art that believers create] is one which hinders honesty. They think that inevitably the writer, instead of seeing what is, will only see what he believes. It is perfectly possible, of course, that this will happen. Ever since there have been such things as novels, the world has been flooded with bad fiction for which the religious impulse has been responsible. The sorry religious novel comes about when the writer supposes that because of his belief, he is somehow dispensed from the obligation to penetrate concrete reality. He will think that the eyes of the Church or of the Bible or of his particular theology have already done the seeing for him, and that his business is to rearrange this essential vision into satisfying patterns, getting himself as little dirty in the process as possible. . . . But the real novelist, the one with an instinct for what he is about, knows that he cannot approach the infinite directly, that he must penetrate the natural human world as it is. The more

sacramental his theology, the more encouragement he will get
from it to do just that.[10]

The creativity of the Christian storyteller is a disciplined creativity: this creativity emerges from the tension between keen attentiveness to the facts of events and belief in the reality of grace. To
sacrifice one side of that tension for the sake of the other cheapens
the art of Christian storytelling. Kate DiCamillo, who is renowned
for her children's stories, gives her own testimony to the unparalleled
importance of seeing well for telling a good story, even outside of
an explicitly religious context: "What I discovered is that each time
you look at the world and the people in it closely, imaginatively,
the effort changes you. The world, under the microscope of your
attention, opens up like a beautiful, strange flower and gives itself
back to you in ways you could never imagine. . . . Writing is seeing.
It is paying attention."[11]

Once again, there is a connection here to the example of our
astronauts learning to see and speak as geologists. Before they could
exercise the creativity required for deep seeing and meaningful
speech, they had to study the basics, they had to learn what to look
for, and they had to see well what was presented to them. In large
part, this relates to the priority of content: those who seek to craft
and share a story of grace must first humbly and diligently give their
attention to what they have received. In the words of Simone Weil,
"Attention is the rarest and purest form of generosity."[12] We can thus
say that it is the "discipline of generosity" that comes before and is
the foundation of true creativity.

Style is already present here, at least implicitly. As we discussed
in the previous chapter, one cannot see grace *as grace* without a willingness to see.[13] Grace is not some *thing* that is transferred but always
an act of communication, a personal and indeed dialogical reality.
This means that there is a "style" to grace—"it" is freely given so "it"
may be freely received, in such a way that God the communicator

makes himself intelligible to the recipient. The communication of grace originates in an act of divine humility whereby the recipient—God's creature—may come to know, love, and respond to this gift. Grace is at once God making himself known *and* God giving the recipients the space and means to know God and, moreover, to know themselves as ones who are thus known by God. In this way, the grace that we come to see is less a blinding light than it is light bent through a prism. That prism is God's humility. God's humility bends God's imperceptible brilliance and makes it visible, so that we may come to know God by faith that seeks understanding. God's humility is the light by which we learn to see (see Ps 36:10).

Style is about creativity, and creativity is concerned with communication: to take what is heretofore unknown and make it known to someone else. The creativity necessary for communicating a story shapes, forms, orders, and narrates what was in some way previously indeterminate and even invisible. Ultimately, the finished story is the embodiment of the inbreathing of a particular experience and the exhaling of one's assent to this experience as one of grace. To state this again according to the themes of vision and light, it is the expression of how one has come to see along a certain beam of light.[14] The mystery of grace is in the exchange between what is received and how one responds; it is, again, a dialogical reality.

The freedom of creativity is never reckless. Already in identifying a story worthy of being told, the faculty of memory is performing a creative exercise. It is easy to confuse memory with mere recalling and recounting, as if the act of remembering had to do with the objectively neutral retrieval of events fixed in the past. We might assume that these events—these facts—are just *there* as independently whole objects that the mind might pull into the present, using something like the mechanical claw in that money trap of an arcade game where you reach down for stuffed animals and mini basketballs. But if we think more deeply about the way in which memory works, we begin to discover something altogether different. We *never* just pull up past experiences as discrete facts as if we were in a "presuppositionless" position when we do so. Instead, our faculty of memory is *already* shaped in some way and is involved in the process of being further shaped when we begin searching for past experiences to recall in the present. When we go in search of something, not only what we are looking for is important but also *how* we choose to look.[15] One could look for the events from his parents' divorce in a posture of scorn and anger that will shape what he finds, or he could look for them with a posture of humble wonder bent toward a desire to discover a beauty that was hidden in the form of pain and confusion—that is, he could look sympathetically. On the basis of the very way in which one seeks to remember one's own experiences, the creativity that becomes a "style" is already emerging. The humility to look in wonder—seeking in order to understand— reflects God's own humility in communicating in grace. For the sake of cultivating this way of seeing, a mentor assists mentees in the formation and exercise of remembering so that the light of faith illumines their seeing.

The work of mentoring and teaching is not limited to helping the storyteller remember; rather, the mentor guides the storyteller in the difficult work of expressing the mystery of grace.[16] How does one speak of suffering and healing in a way that is shaped by and responsive to the Gospel? How does one express grace in the depths of sorrow and loss? How does one recognize God's work in one's own successes or achievements? What symbols relate grace to those who did not share one's experience but will receive a story about the experience? With just this short list of questions, we might already begin to imagine how instruction in the reading of the Psalms, reflection on the works of mercy, or immersion into spiritual practices such as the examen or lectio divina will help students not only "see" better but also begin to "speak" well.

"Style"—as I am calling it here—has to do with the "way" or "the manner in which" a story is told. The most bare-bones news report or historical data entry is concerned with just recording the facts (and even these are never wholly objectively neutral undertakings), but these are very far from the telling of a story. In brief, the style conforms itself to the message—that is, the content—even while it makes that message (or content) present. If the content of a story is truly the embodiment of grace, then the appropriate style of presentation is one that makes that grace present. And if grace has to do not with some *thing* but inextricably with *a person* who has come to know that she is known by God, then the personality—that is, the *personal* expression—of this person (the storyteller) must be present in the expression of the story. You represent your whole self when you tell a story.

In preserving the historical particularity of moments of grace, the storyteller preserves the presence of at least two "persons" simultaneously: God and oneself. In and through the story, the storyteller declares, "God knows me in this way, and this is how I came to know this way of being known." In saying this, the storyteller says something real about God and practices saying the only truly necessary thing about oneself: "This is who I am; I am the one God knows," or as Pope Francis claimed, "I am one who is looked upon by the Lord."[17]

4. Modify It for Your Audience

Every act of storytelling is an act of personal communication. More to the point, in the act of telling a story a form of communion is sought between speaker and listener (or reader). A story is never mere data passing from one node to the next because it also always contains and presents storytellers' own ways of remembering and speaking in their art of communication. If I tell you a story of how I experienced forgiveness, you will receive much more than a statement about past events; you will receive the gift of who I am as the one who experienced that forgiveness along with a personal expression of how I came to see and know myself in some way through this experience. On the flip side, though, when I tell *you* my story, I am handing this story over to you as a particular person (or group of persons), and thus in order to make this an act of communication between persons, I must seek to account for who you are and how you will be able to receive what I hope to give. The audience matters to the way a storyteller tells a story.

Let me offer two analogies to better illustrate this point. In the first instance, we might think about the duty of a teacher. In regard to a particular lesson, the teacher is in possession of some knowledge or understanding to which the pupils themselves are not yet privileged. The teacher's task is to impart this knowledge or share this understanding with the students in such a way that some measure of the teacher's own knowledge and understanding is given to the students so they themselves may come to possess it as their own. If I am the teacher, what matters most is not that "I teach *this* lesson" but rather that "I teach *you* as my student." I may be a leading expert in the subject at hand, but if I cannot discern and act on behalf of the way in which you, my student, will be able to learn what I desire to teach you, then my act of teaching will not be successful. To teach *you*, I must concern myself with not only *what* I must teach but also *how* you will learn best. *You* make a difference to how *I* teach.

As another example, let's imagine I am throwing a surprise birthday party for you, in which case it would be foolish to think only about what I like best. In fact, if I really intend to make this party a gift for you—to honor you—I will think deeply and creatively about what will communicate care for you as well as for the guests that will share in celebrating you. If clowns delight me but terrify you, a party in a clown-filled funhouse will not communicate to you what I hope to express: that I care about and celebrate *you*.

My act of creativity in planning your party must build upon the discipline of knowing and seeking to care for who you are and what brings you joy.

Stories of grace offer to others the "good" the storyteller found and how he found it, "like one beggar telling another beggar where he found bread."[18] When our Notre Dame Vision Mentors craft their stories of grace for the high school students who will receive them, there may be elements of the story that only a college student would understand, and so they have to translate those elements into a form that a high school student will understand. In some instances, it is as simple as describing a college dance in terms resembling a high school dance, while in other instances it might mean speaking tactfully and discretely about misadventures in sexual intimacy. In any case, the storyteller is responsible for including only the pertinent details, those that are important to the story itself and that aid the listeners in their understanding. Teachers, ministers, and mentors are therefore responsible for assisting the storyteller in gauging the appropriate level of detail as well as what details are extraneous to a story. If the story has to do with what happened at someone's house when his parents were out of town, details about the parents' trip to the Greek isles are not essential and will in fact be distracting to the story at hand. The key question is, what do my listeners need in order to receive this story? Similarly, a teacher might ask herself what her students need in order to learn, and someone throwing a party for a friend might ponder what his friend actually likes.

Thinking about one's audience and modifying the way in which the story is crafted accordingly bears some resemblance to what I discussed earlier in terms of the importance of "seeing" the facts of the potential story—the "stuff" of what happened. Paying attention is always an act of generosity, whether to events or to people. In this case, the act of generosity is directed toward one's listeners and potential listeners to discern what they need in order to receive this story and what, in the end, will do them good. While it is certainly true that telling stories of grace is also good for the storyteller, to act toward that end first of all would be to make the act of storytelling a self-serving affair. A crucial dimension of the grace in sharing a story of grace is exercising the charity to give what you have found and even created for the sake of someone else.

To underscore this point, let's return again to two of the authors we featured in the previous chapter: Marilynne Robinson and Flannery O'Connor. In that passage I shared from Robinson's *Gilead*, the narrator, John Ames, remembers the experience he had as a boy when he glimpsed the surprising beauty of the Kansan plain where his grandfather was buried. Even before he writes about this experience for the sake of his own son to whom the letters that make up Robinson's book are written, Ames felt compelled to share the recognition of that surprising beauty with his father, in the midst of the event itself. Here is Ames's remembrance of how he invited his father to see what he himself had already seen: "I wanted my father to see it, but I knew I'd have to startle him out of his prayer, and I wanted to do it the best way, so I took his hand and kissed it. And then I said, 'Look at the moon.' And he did."[19] Notice how at one and the same time the younger Ames is attentive to what he wants to share and to the person with whom he wants to share it. He doesn't want to startle his father since he recognizes that his father is praying, so he acts delicately and gently, kissing his father's hand and then speaking his words. It was "the best way" for him to lead his father to see what he himself was seeing, and in the end, it seems to have been effective. His father acknowledges the beauty and says he is glad to know that beauty could exist in such a place.

For Flannery O'Connor, the challenge, as usual, is not so much in figuring out how to gently awaken her readers to see something already apparent but in shocking her readers into seeing beyond how they tend to see things in their own settled complacency. In a world and in a particular culture where symbols have lost their meanings (and religious symbols most of all), O'Connor has to appeal to a deeper sensitivity that is often buried under the rubble of social conventions and furtive prejudices. In the same essay we cited above, O'Connor writes,

> When I write a novel in which the central action is a baptism, I am very well aware that for the majority of my readers, baptism is a meaningless rite, and so in my novel I have to see that this baptism carries enough awe and mystery to jar the reader into some kind of emotional recognition of its significance. To this end, I have to bend the whole novel—its language, its structure, its action. I have to make the reader feel, in his bones if nowhere else, that something is going on here that counts. Distortion in this case is an instrument; exaggeration has a purpose, and the whole structure of the story or novel has been made what it is because of belief. This is not the kind of distortion that destroys; it is the kind that reveals, or should reveal.[20]

O'Connor's mode differs from Robinson's, but the acts are similar in kind. Each author testifies to the importance of discerning the particular needs of the one to whom she seeks to communicate something important. When Robinson speaks of John Ames gently calling his father to attention, she seems to be also speaking to how she is gently calling us (her readers) to attention.[21] When O'Connor more blatantly speaks of the importance of writing aslant in relation to what would normally be expected, she is speaking to what she perceives to be the need of the majority of her audience to break from how they already tend to think and imagine. Though I do not mean to suggest that stories of grace should include "distortion" and "exaggeration" as do O'Connor's own fictional stories, I do think that elements such as humor, passion, and metaphors function similarly within a personal (rather than fictional) story of grace.

By modifying how your story is crafted for the sake of the particular audience with whom you will share your story, you respect a fundamental truth of every story of grace: it is a story you give to someone else as a gift. To come to recognize grace is to come to recognize something good, something true, and something beautiful, even and especially when that goodness, truth, and beauty exceed or confound what you would have otherwise expected. Grace is God communicating with his beloved creature, so sharing a story of grace is one of the ways in which we share with one another the significance of that act of communication. To care for the needs and the good of those with whom you share such a story is also a way of recognizing the way in which God cares for your own good: always with special attention and personal insight.

5. Ensure There Is Sufficient Closure

We can no sooner finish speaking about stories of grace being gifts we give to others than we must also acknowledge that there is a cost to giving such gifts. Moreover and especially in regard to young people, there are some gifts that they cannot yet (or perhaps ever) afford to give. To this end, I want to uphold the importance of ensuring sufficient closure for any story that one seeks to tell to others. This principle intends to protect the storyteller from causing oneself undue harm—emotional, psychological, social, and spiritual—in the course of telling a story. This principle is also born of the understanding that in many cases, one needs time and distance from an experience in order to tell the story about the experience in a healthy and responsible fashion.

"Sufficient closure" is nothing like a scientific measurement. Prudential judgment is required to determine if closure is sufficient or not. Storytellers must honestly consider what the personal cost of sharing a story will be as well as whether they have some measure of control over the story or whether, alternatively, the story is controlling them. No one is ever required to share a story of grace, even though the need or opportunity for sharing a particular story may be greater or lesser depending on the occasion. While I won't presume to be able to offer an exhaustive list of questions that one must ask oneself before sharing a story, I do think this short list offers some helpful guidance:

- Am I interested in telling this story more because of what it will do for me or because of what it will do for others? (If the former outweighs the latter, there is reason for caution.)

- Do I need to share personal information about other people in this story? If so, are they aware, do I have their permission, and is there any harm (emotional, psychological, social, or spiritual) that might come to them because I am going to tell this story? Otherwise, can I protect their identities?

- Am I seeking reassurance or healing for myself by telling this story? If so, have I already sought appropriate help elsewhere, such as through counseling or spiritual direction?

- If there is a wound involved in this story (of whatever kind), is that wound still raw, or has it started to heal or scar? (The former is a sign that it is not time to share this story.)

- Have I first told this story to those people who would expect to hear about this experience from me directly and perhaps privately?

- Can I recognize the grace in this story? If so, how would I explain this grace in two sentences or less? (Crafting the story can be an exercise in searching for grace; telling the story is an exercise of communicating what you found, not primarily of continuing to search.)

- In what way is there closure to the experience about which I am sharing? (Closure does not mean one is no longer affected by the experience but rather means there is perspective, some distance, and a degree of understanding.)

• Why is this a story worth telling?

I offer but one example of the importance of sufficient closure from my own experience. When my father told me that my paternal grandfather was dying, I drove from Indiana to New Jersey to see him in the hospital. My younger brother and I spent a good deal of time with him in the hospital on the last night that we saw him alive. As we were finally leaving the room, my brother was in front of me and walked out first, but I slowed down and turned around instead of following him into the hallway. I returned to my grandfather's bed, traced the sign of the cross on his forehead, and prayed over him. I had never prayed with or over my grandfather before—in fact, I had never seen him pray himself. The next morning, I drove back to Indiana, arriving just in time to lead an evening retreat with some of the college students with whom I worked. When addressing the group that evening, I felt compelled to say something about that experience of saying good-bye to my grandfather and, especially, the mysteriousness of praying over him. I hesitated, though, and, I realized later, for good reason. At that time, I did not have a story to share for their good. I certainly did have something that I needed to share with someone—my wife, my spiritual director, and my close friends—but not with that particular group of people for whom I was in the position of educating and forming. I was still very much in the moment; I did not have sufficient closure. The wound was raw, I could not explain what the grace was, and had I shared that inchoate story I would have been doing so more for myself than for my listeners. It was only some ten years later that I felt I could hand that story over to others in a way that both communicated grace and served their own good. When I started telling that story (including in an *America* magazine article in November 2015),[22] I did so only after sustained reflection on the meaning of praying for the dying and the dead, the significance of memories, and the relationship and distinction between my respective knowledge of my grandfather and my grandmother in the light of faith. Granting myself the gift of time, of patience, and of reflection served my own best interests as well as those of my eventual audience. When there was some closure to that experience, I was in a position to share it as a gift for others through the telling of a story.

6. Embrace Natural Emotions

John 11:35 is the one verse of scripture that everyone is capable of memorizing: "Jesus wept." Jesus had just returned to Bethany upon the summons of Mary and Martha because their brother and his friend, Lazarus, had died. The most memorable part of this episode is indisputably that Jesus raised Lazarus from the dead, but we would do well to remember that before the revelation of Jesus' divine power there was first a revelation of his humanity. Jesus wept as we weep; he felt the loss of his beloved friend. To tell the story of Jesus and Lazarus without that short verse impoverishes the story itself because that verse helps communicate the fullness of humanity that was united to the fullness of divinity in the person of Jesus. In Bethany, Jesus embraced natural emotions.

When communicating an experience of grace, one of two competing tendencies can impoverish the story itself. The first tendency is to neglect the human realities of the experience in an attempt to overemphasize a miraculous event in the form of divine intervention. The second tendency is to overdramatize (or maybe even underdramatize) the emotional pull of the story in an effort to appeal to the listeners and convince them of the story's importance. We have responded to the first tendency already with the extended treatment of the importance of the content—the "stuff"—of the experience itself, _____ ich the story emerges. In response to the second tendency,

I propose this principle of "embracing natural emotions" in order to resist the urge to embellish while also accepting the authentic emotional quality of a given story. John the Evangelist observed Jesus' embrace of natural emotion at Bethany, and he did so with the shortest verse in all of scripture.

There is something commonsensical to this principle of storytelling. A story about the death of a parent or the struggle with depression will naturally include and potentially evoke different emotional energy than, say, a story about breaking the habit of looking for validation through Facebook "likes." This recognition neither exalts the former stories nor demeans the latter; rather, it respects that the human particularities of each respective story are distinctive and, in all likelihood, correspond to different emotional valences. Not only would overdramatizing a comparatively less emotionally charged experience irritate the sensibilities of the story's teller and receiver alike, but also underdramatizing the experience of losing a parent or battling mental illness would cut against the revelation of the depth of humanity with which God's grace is always concerned. In this case, responding to the humility of God's grace entails humbly accepting whatever emotions are natural to an experience and appropriate to the story about that experience.

One of the most common complaints from those who participate in retreats—or even those who offer them—is that the personal stories that retreat leaders share are collectively too emotional and, in fact, perhaps somewhat inauthentic in that regard. From the perspective of someone who is tasked with offering such a witness, there is often a sense of insecurity about the significance of the story you will share when compared to the perceived significance of the stories of others, especially those whose stories are naturally more emotional. What happens when this insecurity is indulged is that the richness and diversity of the human experience is homogenized, leaving something like a caricature of humanity in its place. The truth is that there are myriad emotional levels to the fullness of the human experience as embraced and revealed in the fullness of grace.

Skilled photographers pay close attention to all the details of a landscape, while skilled poets work their craft in between the peculiarities of their subjects and the specific innovative possibilities of language. Wine connoisseurs train their palettes to discern small variations, while baseball connoisseurs delight in the movement of catchers who routinely back up potential errant throws to first base. If every photograph, poem, wine review, and baseball article sought to portray the same level of drama and emotion, not only would the art and the artist suffer, but also the audience would miss out on the opportunity to glimpse and learn to appreciate the subtle complexity of even the simplest things.

When we share stories of grace, we are communicating that "Jesus wept" is important to the story of his raising of Lazarus. Communicating the emotions natural to a story with the appropriate level of emotion in the storytelling itself serves this end. Taking grace more seriously necessarily entails taking humanity more seriously, and the inverse is also true. Stories of grace are not supposed to abide in a framework of competitive emotionalism; rather, they invite the delicate and discerning skillfulness of artists for the sake of the integrated education of the hearts, minds, and tastes of the audience.

7. Pray and Practice

For good reason one might criticize me for placing this principle at the end of the line, especially in regard to the first part of this principle: "pray." How could a chapter devoted to recommending principles for crafting stories of grace start with anything other than a recommendation to pray, let alone leaving that recommendation for last? Perhaps even more surprising than the apparent disordering of my priorities in this chapter is the fact that I fully agree with this critique: prayer should indeed be the first, most common, and final act in the process of crafting such a story. Why didn't I place this principle first, then? Because I hoped to thicken our notion of prayer before treating it explicitly.

I would like to focus on three biblical prayers in order to gather up all the ways we have already been exploring prayer without explicitly mentioning it. The first comes from the Gospel of Mark, where the father of the boy whom Jesus heals of muteness confesses, "I do believe, help my unbelief" (Mk 9:24). It would be difficult to find a more honest prayer in all the millions of pages devoted to prayer over the millennia. In one and the same breath, this father—a burgeoning disciple—proclaims faith and begs for faith. In his proclamation, this man already acknowledges he is involved in a relationship that opens him to more than he is by himself. He believes in a power not his own, he trusts in Jesus standing before him, and he identifies himself as a believer. In his petition, then, he acknowledges there is more wisdom for him to gain, more sight for him to acquire, and more trust for him to exercise. He is like a man in a dark toolshed who is standing in the beam of light and asking that he may learn to see what the light shows him. When someone sets out to find a story of grace in one's own life, this person is already acting in faith, but in the search itself he is also begging that he may come to understand what he already believes, even if that belief is tentative.

The second prayer is one to which I have already alluded: "In your light we see light" (Ps 36:10). As Marilynne Robinson contemplated in those complementary scenes in *Gilead* that we examined in the last chapter, there is a beauty to creation that we often fail to recognize, and even when we do catch a glimpse, the glimpse makes the beauty seem temporary: "for a moment or a year or the span of a life."[23] That beauty is unseen not because God hides it but because, for one reason or another, we are blind to it. John Ames has to learn to see the grace of communion across death on the stark Kansan plain, and in O'Connor's "Revelation," Ruby Turpin

...ɔt be shocked to consider how neighbors and servants alike are brothers and sisters in a parade toward everlasting life. The psalmist's prayer—which here is an act of praise—is the movement of assent that confesses that "the true light" (Jn 1:9) is first of all God's way of seeing and that we learn to see truly when we learn to see on God's terms. Levi becomes Matthew when he looks along the light of the Lord's gaze. In that light, a new order emerges and everything is different. To see an experience as a story of grace is to see the whole experience anew—in God's light.

The third and final prayer is likewise one to which I already drew attention: "Lord, open my lips; my mouth will proclaim your praise" (Ps 51:17). Why search for, craft, and tell stories of grace at all? We do so to share in the good work that God is doing in the world, personally and compassionately. Sharing in this work is also, at the same time, about allowing God's grace to change who you yourself are as the one who speaks. All acts of faith demand the humble petition to receive the Lord's goodness, while all ways of seeing aright in the world necessitate the gift of God's light. Furthermore, all words of praise—which speak to God and communicate goodness, truth, and beauty to others—rely upon the Word of God first of all. God speaks his Word, and in this Word we are given the freedom to respond and to do so creatively. Praise is never reducible to passing along what we have received; praise always requires responding to what we have received in gratitude, in trust, and in wonder. God's speaking teaches us how to speak well.

Because we as disciples start with Christ and not by assuming absolute knowledge of our own experiences, we are always students of our own experiences. Finding, crafting, and telling our stories of grace is therefore as much a process of learning and of discovery as it is a process of giving gifts to others. The priority of prayer is fundamental: to ultimately share a story of grace, we must always begin with, persist in, and end with the prayer that the God who knows us better than we know ourselves will teach us how to believe, how to see, and how to speak (cf. Rom 8:27).

By praying, we trust that God always makes the first move. But just because God always moves first doesn't mean we don't move; in fact, the tremendous gift of God's movement for us—in creation, redemption, and sanctification—is that we learn how to move with and in God's own love. Just like a ballet dancer or second baseman, learning to move harmoniously in the grand design requires practice. As I stated at the beginning of this chapter, growth in discipleship is oriented to becoming ever more mature, capable, and creative dialogue partners in faith. By practicing telling stories of grace—as well as receiving the stories of others—we participate in the Spirit's work of training us in holiness. Grace will never negate nature; rather, it will heal, strengthen, and perfect nature. Grace doesn't just work *on us* but also *with us*, and in that work "we don't do nothing." In this case, with stories of grace, the considerable "not nothing" we do is to practice remembering, practice attentiveness, practice crafting, practice speaking, practice posture, practice revision, practice responding to guidance, and practice gift giving. A story of grace comes from God, and a story of grace becomes your own as you share it. Prayer and practice respect this tension.

In specific terms, the one crafting a story of grace should embrace all the practices of good writing and, if the story is to be shared orally, good speaking. In terms of writing, the storyteller should brainstorm, write an outline, compose drafts, revise and edit, and elicit feedback from teachers, ministers, or mentors. Though a story of grace is not the same as writing a paper for school, the elements of good composition still apply. The creativity of the storyteller is channeled through the disciplines of learning how to say things well, how to communicate clearly, how to appeal to your audience, and how to allow the structure, content, and style of what you compose to serve the end of communicating well.

Likewise, when a story is to be shared orally, the storyteller should practice actually delivering the story. While full memorization may not be necessary—and having a script or at least substantive notes or an outline to reference is more or less essential for most storytellers—it is important that storytellers become comfortable with and confident in the story they are telling, knowing well what they are going to share and how they are going to share it. Sharing the story in advance with friends or mentors allows storytellers to practice good storytelling. This practice allows a storyteller to identify weak spots in the story where clarity is obscured or to address issues with one's own delivery in regard to pace or volume. All of this practice—in writing and in speaking—is part of the disciplined creativity of one who is learning to move with the grace that is itself the primary subject of the story.

Even with the most exquisite regimen of practice, the entire process for those who are working on stories of grace remains saturated in prayer. I recommend praying the Psalms, because the Psalms (along with the rest of scripture) teach us how to speak by schooling us in the images and grammar of salvation. After all, Jesus himself prayed the Psalms, and the Church organizes the Liturgy of the Hours according to the Psalter. I also recommend spending time in eucharistic adoration, because adoration challenges us to gaze upon someone other than ourselves and to practice listening before speaking. I have already mentioned the importance of journaling in connection with the task of remembering well, but I would also recommend writing letters from yourself to God or, alternatively, from God to yourself. This form of creative journaling—which, I must admit, even strikes me as bordering on hokey—accentuates the dialogical nature of speaking of grace and furthermore encourages extreme thoughtfulness from the start. Last but not least, frequent participation in the sacramental and liturgical life of the Church aids one in trusting in and speaking about grace. The Church teaches us the whole mystery of grace operating in the world through the movements of its own life.[24]

To pray as students of our own lives, we ask God to teach us how to believe, how to see, and how to speak. To that end, John Henry Newman speaks of a memory that recognizes God's action in faithfulness and gratitude:

> Let us thankfully commemorate the many mercies He has vouchsafed for us in time past, the many sins He has not remembered, the many dangers He has averted, the many prayers He has answered, the many mistakes He has corrected, the many warnings, the many lessons, the much light, the abounding comfort which He has from time to time given. Let us dwell upon times and seasons, times of trouble, times of joy, times of trial, times of refreshment. How did He cherish us as children![25]

Newman is inviting his listeners (and readers) not just to see but also to see in a certain way. He encourages them to look for God's mercy, for the signs of accompaniment in good times and in bad, and for the ways in which God has acted through soothing, chastising, and transforming alike. Newman knows that when he tries to remember his own past and look forward to his own future, there will be some light guiding his seeing. As a disciple and as a teacher of disciples, he begs that he may learn to see in God's light, for memory is never neutral. The light of memory is what enabled Saint Matthew to understand that time when someone barged into the room while he and his friends were counting their money as the decisive encounter with the Lord who looked upon him mercifully and renewed his life. John Henry Newman knows about the importance of this light, as does Pope Francis. For those who will find, craft, and tell stories of grace, that discovery awaits.

On Good Listening

Formation in and for stories of grace is obviously not just for the speaker but also, and indeed ultimately, for the listeners. Every story of grace is, for the teller, already an experience of communion with the God who speaks and invites a response. When shared with others, every story of grace also becomes an opening to communion between the storyteller and the audience, who are learning together how to dialogue in the grammar of grace. When we find ourselves on the receiving end of such a story—or, furthermore, when we are in the position of preparing others to listen to these stories—we have a responsibility for being "good listeners" who open ourselves to grace, which, as we know, often outstrips our expectations.

Every once in a while, someone else's story of grace will resemble your own experience very closely. The storyteller's topic will align with your experience (sibling rivalry, struggles with pornography, dealing with a chronic illness, growing through a prayer practice, etc.). The arc of the narrative will be familiar, and many of the details may even line up. When this happens, it is rather easy to hear this person's story as speaking to you for your own benefit. While receiving stories from those with whom you share common experiences is wonderful and sometimes necessary, the benefit of stories of grace for the listeners is not limited to these relatively infrequent occasions.

Listeners should be prepared and guided to receive all stories of grace as symbols of what it is like to look upon the particularities of life in God's light. We are all so conditioned to look only for the entertainment value of what we encounter, for the wow factor, or for trying to "get to the point" (as Internet reading often trains us to do) that we become blind to the light in which someone has come to see and now share this story. With stories of grace, becoming sensitive to this light is of paramount importance to the listener. If someone is sharing a story about the disappointment of being rejected from a college or losing a job, how is it that they are now sharing this as a story of grace? What have they come to see that they perhaps didn't see before? What must it be like to see an experience like this in such a manner? In receiving and reflecting upon these stories in such a way, the listeners must exercise the discipline to listen to what the storyteller is actually saying rather than what they would have already assumed that someone telling a story such as this would say. You may expect that someone who has experienced rejection will say that the rejection was a "blessing in disguise" and that "God had other plans" that were better than one's original plans. Well, something like that may be true, but it may also be the case that the rejection just stung, that the storyteller hasn't shaken the feeling of losing something with that dream school or job, and yet, even in the midst of loss and pain, the light of grace has shone upon them. You could imagine how important this type of disciplined listening becomes when the story is about the death of a loved one, where a listener's interpretation that the death was, in the end, a good thing—that it "happened for a reason"—would be unjust and unfair to the storyteller who experienced this loss. Christ has made even death into a site for grace, not by erasing death but by allowing life to be communicated through it. For the one who lost a parent, a friend, or a spouse, death still hurts even as grace heals, strengthens, and restores what has been lost.

If nothing else, those of us who receive others' stories of grace should cultivate gratitude. Perhaps the experience storytellers share does not align with ours, and perhaps we cannot quite discern how the light of grace is operative in the story; even then, we do well to recognize that the storytellers are making themselves vulnerable in some way, are sharing a part of themselves with us, and, in the end, are trying to give us a gift. Listening closely, trying to understand, and saying "thank you" are the most basic responsibilities of those of us who receive the stories of others.

When we listen well to others we exercise that same cherished capacity that makes us docile to the movements of grace itself: the capacity for paying attention. To return to the words of Simone Weil: "Attention is the rarest and purest form of generosity."[26] What happens when you pay attention is not just that you practice generosity but also, over time and with repetition, that you actually become a more generous person. In receiving others' stories of grace with attentiveness, we give space in our hearts and minds for another person to commune with us, just as—when we pay attention to how God sees the world and sees us—we open ourselves up to becoming renewed in grace. Prayer itself is attentiveness to God, so every act of attentiveness is already practice for praying well. In the giving and receiving of stories of grace, we join together in practicing attentiveness to the beauty of creation that God sees as *good* (Gn 1:4, 10, 12, 18, 21, 25) and even *very good* (Gn 1:31).

Chapter 3

Speaking of Light

Studying the Splendor and Language of Grace

Though stories of grace may concern life-altering conversion experiences, these stories are not limited to those climactic moments. Being "wowed" by larger-than-life events and shockingly dramatic movements is thrilling, and there are times when circumstances align in such a way that moments such as these burst upon the scene. But desiring to give our attention only to what stuns and impresses makes us into something like adrenaline junkies, who seek bigger and bigger thrills in order to get a rush. If we set our hearts and our expectations in this way, then we end up with dulled rather than heightened sensitivity to grace. We would demand grace on our terms rather than allowing grace to renew us on its own terms, that is, in God's light.

Maybe Saint Augustine is partially to blame for our fascination with the dramatic in stories of grace; then again, maybe he's not. After all, it is often the readers and interpreters of his *Confessions* that narrow the view of his conversion to the moment in the garden where he takes and reads scripture at the mysterious prompting of a child and then throws himself down under a tree. The quick summary of his story tells of his sudden conversion from lust to chastity or pride to humility. Yet to sever this moment—even if only in our memories—from the story of the preceding books of his work, all

71

of which contain numerous particular stories, is to trade away the full richness of Augustine's testimony. Though his text is ultimately about the remaking of his entire life in the light of God's mercy, that project is the furthest thing from "Instant Uplift,"[1] since Augustine testifies to the balm of mercy seeping into all the nooks and crannies of the concrete particularities of his life over a long period of time. In fact, even in the momentous Book 8 of *Confessions*, we discover not Augustine's story of conversion as if a thunderbolt empowers his turning all at once but rather a series of stories that woo him and prepare the way for that climactic turn.

If we look closely, we can find up to eight stories within Book 8 that precede the drama of Augustine's turn in the garden, and each of these stories is ultimately drawn into Augustine's personal story of grace. The first story from which Augustine benefits comes from a man whom Augustine held in high regard. Simplicianus was the godfather of Ambrose—the bishop of Milan—and the one to whom Augustine entrusts his own difficulties of finding his way in the world. Listening attentively to how Augustine tells of his experience, Simplicianus notes how Augustine read certain philosophical books, which were translated into Latin by a famous rhetorician and convert to Christianity: Victorinus. Simplicianus uses this opening to instruct Augustine, not in terms of the intellectual arguments that Augustine himself always preferred (such as the ones he encountered in those philosophical texts) but through the *story* of the man who translated those texts. The story of Victorinus is one of a celebrated and successful public intellectual who humbled himself to the ministry of the Church in baptism and received the Sign of the Cross upon his forehead in public. Even more, rather than making his profession of faith in private to avoid drawing the ire of the learned elite who would see such a proclamation as a sign of weakness, Victorinus proclaims his faith in public before the learned and unlearned alike. Victorinus commits his heart as well as his mind to the costly task of seeing himself in light of God's mercy through joining others in the body of the Church. In a very particular way, he gave up the desire to be recognized as special in circumstance and exalted in intellect in order to find himself as beloved among other beloved ones in the sight of the Lord.[2]

Now Victorinus's story seems big, like one of those impressive conversion stories that are rare and oftentimes intoxicating. In a way, Victorinus's story *is* one of those stories, but Simplicianus did not tell this story to Augustine to captivate him with entertaining drama; rather, Simplicianus told Augustine this story because it resonated with Augustine's own story, which Simplicianus had already received in inchoate fashion.[3] Augustine himself had long desired public acclaim, to be recognized for his intellectual ability and his rhetorical skills. For Augustine, the single greatest obstacle to accepting the grace he deeply desired—to be known and to know himself accordingly—was his unwillingness to become humble in giving praise to God rather than seeking praise for himself. Victorinus's story was thus a model for his own journey, and Simplicianus, the wise and discerning guide, offered this story to Augustine not to flatter his mind but to appeal to his heart: "On hearing this story I was fired to imitate Victorinus; indeed it was to this end that your servant Simplicianus had related it."[4]

Even with the appropriateness of this story for Augustine's own journey, there is nothing like a neat cause-and-effect relationship between Augustine learning of Victorinus's story and making his own act of faith. In fact, as Augustine tells his own story he moves on to recall how he entered into another conversation and received yet other stories offered for his benefit. The next storyteller is Ponticianus: a man who held an important post at court and who was, like Augustine and his friends, an African. In their conversation, Ponticianus tells of five other figures whose stories pertain to the sort of yielding to grace to which Augustine's own story is building. The

first story is of Antony of Egypt, whose encounter with the text of
the Gospel moved his heart and prompted him to leap toward a new
way of life, selling all he possessed and giving to the poor to follow
Christ (see Mt 19:21). Antony's story finds a place in Augustine's
heart, and Augustine explicitly cites it later at the critical moment
when he himself is "stung into action" in the garden.[5]

Following the story of Antony himself, Ponticianus then tells
the story of two court officials and their wives who themselves experience the grace for conversion in response to encountering the text
of Antony's story.[6] In recounting the stories that Ponticianus tells
about these four people, Augustine is accounting for how his own
movement with grace was modeled after and anticipated by the ways
in which those in Ponticianus's story were themselves moved by Antony's witness. Therefore, what moves Augustine is not only the power
of Antony's story but also the power of the stories of these others
who were themselves moved by Antony's story. It is as if Augustine
receives both the gift of an important story (Antony's) and the gift of
learning how to respond to such a story (in the witness of the court
officials and their wives).

So it is that along with the underlying story of Saint Paul that
runs throughout Book 8 as well as the additional story of yet another
"important person" whom Paul himself converted—the proconsul
Sergius Paulus[7]—this collection of stories shows how Augustine's
own story cannot be reduced to a singular moment removed from
the particular context of his life experience. Looking back upon the
first line of Book 8 in light of the moment of grace that includes all
these other stories, we come to see that the gift of these stories is part
of the mercy the Lord cast upon Augustine: "In a spirit of thank-
fulness let me recall the mercies you lavished on me, O my God;
to you let me confess them."[8] His story includes these other stories,
and his moment of action in response to grace connects to all the
particular experiences he recounts throughout the *Confessions*. Like

the character John Ames in *Gilead*, who reconsiders his Pentecost sermon, the moment of grace in the garden in Milan casts light upon the constancy of grace working throughout and in all the concrete particularities of Augustine's life.[9]

The point here is that commonplace interpretations that present neat and tidy explanations of one of the most famous conversion stories of all time misrepresent the deeply personal nature of how grace moves in and through Augustine's story. It is typical to recall Augustine's story of grace according to the model of a dramatic life-altering event that occurs all at once, such as Saul being knocked down on the road to Damascus and being instantaneously converted to Christ. The problem with this association is not that we fail to distinguish Augustine's story from Paul's but rather that Paul's story is itself glossed over when represented as an example of an instantaneous conversion—or, more to the point, as the paradigmatic model of one. The flash of light, the falling to the ground, and the voice of the Lord speaking to Saul are only one part of the story, like the shock that begins to usher in a new reality. Saul spent three days in blindness, without food or water, and his awakening only occurs once one of the very Christians whom Saul would have persecuted—Ananias—lays hands on the once proud Saul, who humbly accepts not only healing at the hands of this humble man but also baptism and food to revive his strength (see Acts 9:3–19). Moreover, the significance of even this three-day conversion experience remains obscured without knowing the rest of the story of who Saul had been and, in the end, who Paul becomes. Paul's story thus follows the call narratives of other apostles such as Saint Matthew, for whom the grace of conversion reckoned with the story he had been living and led him to the discipleship he was called to embrace. Likewise, the mercy of the Lord came to Augustine as he was—a talented man addicted to prestige—and healed him in part through the stories of other "important men" who learned to humbly rediscover themselves as ones whom the Lord looks upon in mercy.

By attending more closely to even these "great" stories of grace, where the most well-known disciples do ultimately experience life-altering moments of conversion, we see that even these stories are much more personal, much more particular, and much more concrete than we are accustomed to considering. Without seeing the other stories that wooed Augustine, we cannot really see his own story as he presents it for us. The fascination with the thrill of the climax dulls our sensitivity to the sometimes delicate, sometimes subtle, and sometimes peculiar ways in which grace works in, through, and with human life. For those who craft stories of grace as well as for those who receive them, attentiveness to the tremendous personalism of how grace works with the whole of the human experience is of utmost importance, lest we conceive of grace by our own preferences rather than allowing ourselves to grow in grace.

This chapter is dedicated to helping us exercise our perceptivity to the workings of grace. To this end, I will present excerpts from nine different stories of grace as crafted by those with whom we have worked in Notre Dame Vision. If one were to offer a summary of these stories, one might say they are about battling an anxiety disorder, struggling with a loved one's Alzheimer's, absorbing the repercussions of alcoholism, learning from people with mental disabilities, dealing with an eating disorder, fighting against pornography, experiencing forgiveness, renewing one's vocation as a teacher, and wading through the pain of infertility, respectively. By paying close attention to some of the particular aspects of these stories, however, we seek to attune ourselves to what the storytellers are trying to communicate to us about the surprising but also specific ways that grace moved in and through their experiences. The form of deeper listening that we will attempt here is a model for the kind of attentiveness we should foster when we craft our own stories of grace as well as when we lead others to do so or when we prepare listeners to receive stories. In the fragments of the stories to follow, perhaps we can catch a glimpse of how these particular experiences point to the whole complex drama of grace that makes the seemingly mundane shine like transfiguration, if only we have eyes to see.

Reflections of Grace

For each of the excerpts of stories of grace that follow, I will do three things. First, I will provide basic information about the story to set the context for the particular excerpt. Second, I will present the excerpt itself. Third, I will offer some brief commentary on the excerpt to help us attend to some of the elements that the author incorporated in the telling of the story or otherwise to note some of the particular ways in which grace is presented within the story. Of course, the best way to appreciate these stories would be to receive them whole from the storyteller himself or herself, but the set of exercises we shall undertake is comparable to the drills athletes engage in to refine their athleticism and develop fluidity in specific skills. In like manner, I intend for these samples to allow us to focus on certain dimensions of these stories and the craft employed in telling them, in hopes that by treating them we will sharpen our appreciation for the gift that is given in stories such as these. Along with the principles enumerated in the preceding chapter, this collection of excerpts offers valuable guidance for recovering the art of storytelling in order to renew evangelizing efforts in our contemporary situation.

Story 1: "New Pathways" by Ashley Scott

Ashley long self-identified as a worrier well before her efforts to manage and suppress her worries started to fail. Under the pressures of life in college, where multiple responsibilities simultaneously vie for attention, she started to experience physical consequences of her worrying, such as dizziness, chills, and fatigue. After finally confiding in her boyfriend and her parents, she visited a doctor, who tested her and found that nothing was physically wrong, and then started up a relationship with a counselor. The counselor diagnosed Ashley with a moderate form of anxiety. In the course of her work with the counselor, Ashley both learned about her ailment and began the journey toward recovery:

> I learned that when you think, your brain forms small indentations, marking the places where familiar thought patterns make their way through your mind. These indentations make your mind more comfortable with certain—sometimes unhealthy—pathways. My mind has become comfortable with an anxious thought pattern, so that now I have to work harder to create new, deeper indentations, to teach my body and mind to respond differently to potentially stressful situations. . . .
>
> So I began this process of healing. Part of this process requires me to pay closer attention to my thoughts and feelings, especially during times of anxiety. If any of you have ever been told to pay attention to how you feel when you feel awful, you know it isn't a pleasant experience, and everything did not magically turn a corner and become better. The process became rather frustrating: I knew my anxiety was something I should be able to handle, and for some reason I couldn't, or I was doing it the wrong way.
>
> But I started working harder at carving the indentations. I thought often and thought hard, trying to dig them as

deep as possible into my mind. I pushed against the thoughts, and there were days they pushed back just as hard.

But that's when I let God into my struggle. And it hit me. It wasn't my anxiety that was the source of my problems. It was my attitude. I was not loving myself *as I am*, and this lack of love was hindering my ability to love my family, to love my boyfriend, to love my friends, to love God, and to cope with my anxiety. I knew I had to work on changing that. It sounds like a simple idea and a simple practice, but it is so much easier said than done.

How would you describe grace in this story? You might detect grace in the support of Ashley's parents and boyfriend, in the professional care of the counselor, or simply in God entering into her struggle. You might say that grace heals, that grace gives reason for hope, or that grace is what makes the burdens of life bearable. But if we pay close attention to what Ashley is sharing, we may also come to recognize something we might not have otherwise expected: grace works in and through her body, in and through her mind, and in and through her will and her desire.

By paying such close attention to the anxiety that ailed her and precisely how it did so—by impressing indentations into her brain that became channels for ways of thinking—Ashley was also able to speak more clearly and directly about how healing is taking place in her life. In gratitude for what others did for her, Ashley is responding by working hard to be an agent in her own healing. Yet even this work was frustrating, and because she sensed failure in her own efforts, the work of healing became another source of anxiety. And so, in an act of faith, Ashley opens the whole experience more fully to the presence of God.

Part of this openness requires a fundamental change in herself: she has to learn to accept herself as she is, as God's beloved one. The pathway underneath all the other pathways is this one, by which the practice of learning to accept herself as a gift of God powers the healing of her whole self. There is no "Instant Uplift" in this image of grace; rather, in grace Ashley continually rediscovers the courage to change, heal, and most of all, learn how to trust in support for which she herself is not responsible.

Story 2: "Bella" by Emma Fleming

The story that Emma tells happens to begin with a saying that is sometimes used in place of substantive reflection: go with God. While this saying is at heart an invitation to trust, in practice it is often used to foster disengagement. For Emma, who like many of us prefers to be in control, this "easy out" toward relinquishing control was always unappealing, including when her family suffered through her grandfather's slow decline with Alzheimer's disease. In order to cling to control, Emma testifies to resorting to practices of blame as her grandfather became increasingly more difficult to live with and the consequences of his illness intensified. The target for this blame pierced through her grandfather to God, whom she blamed for doing this to her grandfather and her family. The frustration and pain reached its pinnacle on the day her grandfather forgot who she was:

> My heart broke. My grandpa had forgotten who I was. In that instant, my mind was only filled with one thought: *He's gone.* All of our memories together had disappeared from his mind. Our duets at family Christmas parties. Playing princess dress-up and always appointing him the Royal King. The times of being called "Bella Emma," my nickname only used by him. All of this was gone. I was left holding onto a relationship I could not restore. My mom rushed in to try and save the conversation: "Dad, this is Emma, your granddaughter. Bella Emma, remember?" Embarrassed at his confusion,

faking a weak sense of understanding, we went on with our day, and that was the last time I saw him.

I often thought after my grandpa died that I should have been kinder to him. I was so hurtful to Grandpa. I wanted someone to blame for what was happening and especially for the way that his memory loss was hurting me. I took it out on my grandfather when it clearly wasn't his fault. It wasn't anyone's fault. He did not wish to hurt me by forgetting our favorite songs, our memories, or even my name.

Although Grandpa's memory was limited and grew weaker, I've learned to appreciate the one thing he never failed to remember: prayers. My grandpa may not have known what day it was, but he could sit down, place his rosary in his hand, and recite prayers perfectly. Effortlessly. Looking back on this time, I recognize that *this was grace*, a sign of God amidst the suffering. God was peace in Grandpa's tangled mind. God was peace in my weak heart.

Grandpa's battle with Alzheimer's was a part of his life that I could not change. With each step down his path of memory loss, I had to let go of my control over my relationship with him, slowly entrusting him to God. In learning to allow God to carry my grandpa, I also allowed God to carry me.

In the course of her story, Emma actually calls the name of "grace," which that sign of her grandfather at prayer called to mind. There is nothing but increasing frustration and intensifying pain up to this point in the story. In fact, the portrait of grace that Emma paints is one in which suffering can be no less severe even when grace is present. All the same, the recognition of the presence of grace gently turns the whole memory into one in which gratitude becomes possible. This is not gratitude for the disease or for its consequences, nor is it in any way gratitude for the suffering itself. Instead, the gratitude is for the gift of learning in love what it means to "go with God," who would rather carry us than abandon us in times of trial, even when it seems we are being pulled apart from one another. Emma's recognition of grace did not change the facts of the situation, it did not restore her grandfather's memories in a way that she could observe, and it did not stop death. What grace did was provide a light by which Emma sees and, in that light, through which she sees not only her grandfather but also herself.

Story 3: "From Wine to Blood" by Vincent David

Vinnie has always been that guy at the party who isn't drinking and who others therefore occasionally suspect of judging them. By his own admission, this perception is not unfounded. Many times, Vinnie was judging those who drank, especially those who drank to excess, yet his judgment was not first of all about a concern with virtue; rather, it was tied to deep pain in his own life. Vinnie's father is an alcoholic, and when Vinnie was young, his father first disengaged from committed involvement in his family's life and then, ultimately, left them altogether. For a long time, Vinnie has associated the presence of alcohol with the absence of his father, and the pain of that absence results in disgust for the substance in which his father indulged and that, in his sickness, drove him further away from his family. The pain and disgust that Vinnie experienced flooded his life as a dominant theme, so much so that even the contents of the chalice at Mass substantially communicated suffering, sorrow, and blame because its properties were consistent with alcohol:

> Alcohol carried so much anger, so much sadness, and so much pain that for a long time I couldn't drink from the Communion cup at Mass. I could not see that cup as holding the Blood of Christ; all I could see was alcohol. But sometime

this past fall, I started to feel pulled toward that cup. In my prayer, I felt God was prompting me to make a choice about what my life is going to be about: Is my life about the demons that haunt me, or is it about accepting the loving embrace of God, who will fight my demons with me? Deep within I knew that I needed to get past the alcohol and receive the Blood of Christ. I knew I needed the Blood of Christ who died for me, who loves me. Whether it's alcoholic or not is irrelevant. It's *real*.

The Blood of Christ has brought some healing to my relationship with my dad. I still can't say that I have forgiven him completely. I know that any anger I harbor toward him is only hurting me and that I can never really repair my relationship with him unless I forgive him. But just as there's no greater sign of truly real love, there's no greater sign of truly real forgiveness than the Eucharist. God, who is perfect and needs nothing from us, forgives us of every depraved thing we do, every failure to love that we enact, and we are graced with this forgiveness in every Mass through the Eucharist. I haven't completely forgiven my dad, but I see no better way to work toward forgiveness than entering into the most real forgiveness of all.

The question that Vinnie hears at the core of his experience is a question about the underlying truth of the world: Does fear run the world or does love? If it is fear, then the righteous anger and understandable pain of what and how he suffers work together to separate him from another order that would transform his own, one in which alcohol is used to communicate life rather than loss. By the pull toward the cup at Mass, however, Vinnie began to allow his own experience to be recast in a perfect love that drives out fear (1 Jn 4:18).

As with Emma's story above, the love communicated in grace does not remove the elements of suffering and loss; rather, that love begins to transform those elements so that the wounds of neglect slowly become the sites where forgiveness blooms. The power that Vinnie recognizes at work in his story is not first of all his own power; he begins to recognize that the power of a love that exceeds him makes a claim on him, and in doing so it renews his own power, thus reshaping blame into a desire to reconcile. Part of the miracle here is, therefore, the transformation of Vinnie's desire. In one and the same Eucharist, Vinnie finds both the failures of his father and the unrelenting love of God, and by drinking from that cup he allows the latter to meet the former in his own life. Vinnie gives us a view of grace not as the end of a story but as the perpetual beginning of the newness of life.

Story 4: "Just Be" by Sarah Ruszkowski

We live in a fast-paced world. From the time we are children, those of us who are able are taught to do a lot of things all at once and to do them as expeditiously as possible. The ability to multitask is flaunted like a badge of honor, with the more capable among us often exalted as the most valuable, impressive, and worthy of imitation.

As a recent college graduate, Sarah had mastered the art of doing many things at once, of filling her schedule with as many activities as possible, and of spreading out her energies while always maintaining the appearance of holding it all together. In both subtle and not-so-subtle ways, the very same education in which Sarah had been immersed for most of her life qualified her for admission to a prestigious college and helped her to succeed while in the college setting; it is also a kind of cultural education that tends to measure personal worth according to one's ability. When she moved into a L'Arche[10] community in Washington, DC, after her graduation from college, she was immersed in a new education where value is measured in tenderness and togetherness:

And then there is Maria. Maria is "my lady" as I like to call her. She is my rock here. She is a woman of few words, especially when she is eating. She will actually sit in complete silence during a meal (even when it is just the two of us at a restaurant). On one of our first meals out with just the two of us, I was talking enough for the both of us. She calmly looked at me and said, "We can just eat." At first, I was taken aback, and then I could not stop laughing. It was true. We could just be together. I did not have to prove anything to anyone. More than most, Maria knows the power of a smile for a lonely heart. She knows when I need her to hold my hand or just sit next to me. . . .

Maria has taught me how to be present. In L'Arche, our mission is shared life. Our mission is to live life in such a way that everyone in our home—those with disabilities and those without disabilities—know that they are worth it, that they are worthy of God's love. And it doesn't come from grand gestures, big plans, or meticulous schedules. It comes from the fact that you show up every day.

I have been reflecting a lot lately on what it means to "be God's love" [as the theme song for Notre Dame Vision proclaims]. In my life in L'Arche, it is most often seen in silent couch-sitting (together), chaotic twelve-person dinners (together), and awfully harmonized song-belting-out (together). It is so easy for me to become entangled in big notions of what it means to be God's love. But where I have received God's love the most, where I have been able to share it the most, is in those moments when we are just "together." Just being. But that fits, doesn't it? Just "being"? When that phrase was used with me before, my planner, list-making mind would often wonder: Just being *what*? I think I get it a little more now. It's just being the ones God loves.

In the famous beginning to his book *Dependent Rational Animals*, the philosopher Alasdair MacIntyre observes that, by and large, "we are invited, when we think of disability, to think of 'the disabled' as 'them,' as other than 'us,' as a separate class, not as ourselves as we have been, sometimes are now, and may well be in the future."[11] In L'Arche, Maria is teaching Sarah how to be dependent, to be vulnerable, and to recognize her own disability to see herself as more than the sum of her abilities.

If grace sometimes comes as a shock to what we perceive as the ordinary way of things, for Sarah this shock elicited laughter—uncontrollable laughter. Like her namesake for whom laughter signaled the clash between the limitless possibilities of God's desire to give and her own inability to bear children (see Gn 18:9–14), this Sarah is struck by the surprising gift of "just being" together, which exceeds anything she would be able to accomplish or achieve on her own. Maria shocked her, and at first she was "taken aback," but as a result of that shock she began to take herself more lightly and wade into the immeasurable gift of a community that reminds the able-bodied of their humanity through sharing life with those whose value is not limited to the narrow metrics of ability. In Sarah's story, grace first wounds her pride in order to heal her vision with a revelation of communally embodied love.

Story 5: "In Mysterious Ways" by Renée Roden

Bulimia walked into Renée's life when she was a junior in high school. Since then, she has faced the constant struggle of eating healthily. The disordering effects of bulimia upon her body bruise her emotional and psychological well-being, so that the result of the ups and downs of managing this part of her life leads to the experience of humiliation and, most of all, frustration. She wants to eat well, she wants to care for herself, and yet she cannot always do what she wills. In the middle of college, when the disappointments were overwhelming her successes, she found herself in one of those low moments when hope is difficult and the weight of the burden feels too heavy by half:

> I was sitting on the front steps of my dorm. I was having an awful week eating. I'd been doing so well for most of the semester, which was making that week doubly difficult. I just sat there with my head in my hands, soaked in the rain. The only prayer I was praying was, "God, I can't do this. God, I'm not strong enough."
>
> Out of the blue, I heard a voice ask, "Hey, are you okay?"
>
> It took me a moment to realize the voice was directed at me. But then I looked up and saw a guy standing there. So I forced a smile and responded with, "Oh yeah, I'm fine."
>
> As soon as the words were out of my mouth, I knew how ridiculous I sounded. *I was sitting outside—crying—in the rain.* There are a lot of ways to define the word "fine," but that's not one of them.
>
> He looked at me with kind disbelief and said, "Okay. Are you sure?"
>
> "Oh yeah, I'm good. Thanks though."
>
> So he walked away, and I returned to sitting and staring into the rain. Then I heard him turn around. He came back and approached me again. "You look like you could use a hug," he said, and then he gave me a giant bear hug.
>
> I was so overwhelmed by the kindness and love in that hug. I smiled: "Thank you. Thank you so much."
>
> "Whatever it is, I hope it gets better," he said. Then, with a smile of his own, he jogged off into the rain. But that simple moment of grace had completely turned around my night.
>
> I haven't seen the guy since then. One of my friends asked me if he was an angel. I said unless angels wear puffy North Face jackets and basketball shorts and have an earbud in one ear, then no. I think he was just a normal guy who did

something really extraordinary. He extended love to someone
he didn't even know not just once but twice.

A dimension of the grace in this story is so apparent that it
hardly requires saying anything beyond what Renée already said:
grace moved with the searching and resilient kindness of a stranger
who communicated companionship across a gap of understanding.
He didn't know what Renée's wound was, but he knew something
about how to help heal that wound, and he acted.

What is perhaps less apparent is another dimension of grace
that pertains not to the North Face angel but to Renée herself: she
was able to recognize his act as an act of grace, and that recognition
changed her way of seeing. Her way of seeing was certainly altered
for that night—as she attests—but because she later tells this story
as a story of grace, her way of seeing is altered also from the position
of the one who tells this story as her own. What might have otherwise been a memory of frustration and failure became a memory
of hope and companionship. Driven outside into the prison of her
own disappointment, her memory of the experience is not about
imprisonment but rather that "I was in prison and you visited me"
(see Mt 25:36). In grace, the memory of isolation becomes a memory
of visitation. I'm tempted to call that a miracle.

Story 6: "The Casings of the Heart" by Geoffrey Burdell

As if being labeled a "good kid" wasn't pressure enough, Geoff was
labeled the "good Catholic boy," bringing the expectations for moral
flawlessness to a whole new level. It many respects, his behavior and
intentions matched the expectations others had for him, and for
the most part he thrived. When the problem of an unhealthy desire
emerged and intensified, however, the dissonance between how he
felt about his own struggle and how he perceived other people's

expectations of him left him trapped, with seemingly nowhere to turn. "Good Catholic boys" don't get hooked on pornography, or so we might assume. Hemmed in with nowhere to turn outside of himself for fear of disappointing, Geoff struggled interiorly, where shame flourished under its ideal conditions:

> My struggle was something hidden very deep within me, something that I wrestled with in the crevices of my heart, one of the dreariest spots that has ever plagued my conscience. For so long I had wanted to bury my sin and shame within myself, hiding in that isolation forever. But as grace would have it, that all began to change at the end of my sophomore year of college.
>
> My residence hall community was hosting a retreat at the end of the year. At that time, my frustration was weighing especially heavy on my heart and mind since I had been struggling mightily with my problem for the entire year. I felt that the silent burden of my shame and the lack of control I had over my own thoughts and will were becoming increasingly unbearable and discouraging, and I prayed that God would somehow alleviate my pain with this retreat.
>
> As it turns out, the weekend was filled with deep conversations and expressions of solidarity with other men my age, many of whom were struggling in the same way I was. To my great shock and relief, I was *not* the only one fighting this battle. The openness we fostered on this retreat was new to me, and the way that so many of these men humbly admitted their own imperfections and turned in trust to God's mercy for healing was unprecedented in my life. This grace-filled communication pierced me, and I sensed that through this shared encounter perhaps God was priming my heart for a renewed openness to his loving compassion, even and especially in that bleak area of my life that I had considered exempt from him for so long. The faith-filled witness of several other men inspired me to believe that if others could

deal with this problem, trusting in God, then perhaps it was possible for me to do the same.

At a time when Geoff was without courage, he drew courage from the humility of those who made themselves vulnerable. The fact that someone else sharing his pain with you can become the beginning of your own healing is a confounding concept when considered in simply rational terms. Putting your broken leg next to my broken leg doesn't incite the healing process, and the same goes, we might reasonably assume, for other forms of affliction. But since Geoff's suffering wasn't just what he perceived to be his lack of control and the sadness of his habit but was in fact the feeling of isolation, of peculiarity, and most of all of shame, the gift of others sharing their own hidden sorrows with him was precisely the balm for his interior wounds.

The grace of that encounter, where solidarity was formed around shared pain, is so persuasive, so efficacious, that in now sharing his story for the sake of others, Geoff is offering himself in the likeness of the very gift that he received. Thomas Aquinas describes this as "free grace," by which God makes us capable of leading each other into what is good, whole, and healthy.[12] The depth of the mystery of grace to which Geoff testifies is of the merciful Lord who empowers those he heals to become agents in the healing of others and then for those others, in turn, to become agents of healing for others still. In this manner the Lord proclaims himself as "gracious and merciful . . . continuing his love for a thousand generations" (Ex 34:6–7).

Story 7: "The Memory of Communion" by Victoria Kay

Theology is classically defined as "faith seeking understanding." Within the discipline of theology, we might come to assume that this seeking is only or primarily to be undertaken intellectually, as if faith were one piece of knowledge and understanding was the next one to which we were trying to make a connection. All true theology begins in prayer, though, since nothing is ever truly said *about* God that is not first of all said *to* God in response to what God says to us. The reality of faith often precedes what we think about faith, and this truth is at the heart of the sacramental logic of the Church. In the sacraments, we enter into a mystery we do not fully comprehend so that, by abiding there, we might come to understand who we are becoming in the love of God.

When Victoria was in high school, she received a theological education from the theology teacher who also doubled as her history teacher. But just as the journey from faith to understanding is not restricted to the road of the intellect, so Victoria's theological education was not restricted to Mrs. Gerson's classroom. In fact, within that classroom Victoria was aggrieved by the way Mrs. Gerson treated her, demeaning and dismissing her as a student. What Victoria took from that experience was primarily the grudge of one who knows herself to have been offended. It wasn't, therefore, in the classroom that Victoria developed theological insight but when she stood at the front of her parish to distribute the Eucharist. From that perspective and in that action, Victoria came to understand her faith in a God who calls us to share in his one Body:

> As I picked up the host and raised it up reverently before the communicant, I found myself looking eye-to-eye with Mrs. Gerson. I could not believe what was happening. In a moment that seemed to last forever, I felt all the pain, the fury, the hurt, and the hate resurge in my body. Then just as quickly as those feelings had come, they dissipated and sudden peace filled my body when I said the words, "The Body of Christ."

I placed the host—the living God—into her outstretched hands. She said "Amen," made the Sign of the Cross, and then turned down the aisle. I was stunned and didn't know what to think. In an instant, we were no longer student and teacher (with a grudge between us) but rather two believers who had come to eat at the table of Christ. When I looked at her, I still felt the resentment that lingered in my heart, but looking up at the host, I saw Mrs. Gerson for who she really was. In the Body of Christ, I was able to see that Mrs. Gerson was like me: a sinner trying to orient her life toward Christ. As with me, Christ shows his love to her in spite of her sins. And it is Christ's unconditional love given to us in the Eucharist that joins her to me and makes us one in him.

Not unlike Vinnie's story previously, Victoria testifies to the meeting of sin and love, offense and forgiveness, in this one place: the sacrament of the Eucharist. What is striking here is that a theological insight emerges in the practice of the faith, in its very movement. In participating in the logic of God, who hastens to join together those who have been rent asunder, Victoria reimagined herself as one whom the Lord was reuniting to the teacher that she had willfully separated from in enmity, with a legitimate grievance. In the space that Christ opens up in his Body given from the altar, Victoria glimpsed the possibility of a new story growing out of the old one. This belief did not emerge because an argument convinced her; it emerged because an action persuaded her. Beauty is its own argument.

Story 8: "Love Them into Being" by Katlyn Patterson

I teach college, which means that when I finish teaching a class, I can typically go back to my office, close the door, and recuperate in solitude if necessary. I may even have a gap of a day or two between class meetings. High school and grade school teachers enjoy no such luxury; they teach almost the entire day, every day. At the end of the week, even the most joy-filled and passionate teacher is often exhausted and in need of a break. When the last quarter of the school year rolls around, the cumulative effect of all those weeks of hard work—of caring, instructing, correcting, and reiterating—accumulate into a special kind of exhaustion. For Katy Patterson, who viewed her teaching profession as a vocational commitment and who sought to respond to the call of the Gospel in her role as a teacher of science and of theology in a boys' high school in Baltimore, the exhaustion late in the spring was no less considerable, even though she believed deeply in what she was doing:

> "Do I need my lab gear today?" "Will we have homework?" "Can I get my book from my locker?" "Can I go to the bathroom?"
>
> Patience. Some days take a lot of patience. And so I find myself constantly praying for the Holy Spirit's gifts to guide my teaching and care for the students entrusted to me. But when I went to the adoration chapel that night, I was resolved to *not* pray about school. School typically consumes most of my conversations and most of my thoughts during most days. I was determined not to allow school to follow me into my prayer time. But as I sat in front of Jesus in the Blessed Sacrament, I remembered a line I included in a lesson earlier that day: "We have been created out of love and for love." God loved me into being, and it is through allowing this identity to become my mission that I become most fully human. I have been called to love. What I kept hearing during my prayer that day was one simple phrase: "Love them into being."
>
> And so I found myself praying about school, despite my intentions to the contrary. This is my vocation as a teacher:
>
> Love them into being confident.

Love them into being kind.
Love them into being joyful.
Love them into being more fully themselves.
Love them into being with a love that
originates in our Creator and begs to flows
through me.

I realized the grace and the challenge of this prayer as my students and I persevered through another Friday late in the year.

Paul asked me to explain the same problem for the
fourth time. *Love them into being self-advocates.* My tone soft-
ened and (hopefully) conveyed patience instead of frustration.

Mark didn't take notes during eighth period class. *Love
them into being responsible.* I reviewed the material with Mark
again while he was in detention, working with him until he
understood the concept.

Trevor sat in the back of the classroom with his head
propped on his hand, completely uninterested. *Love them into
being included.* I gave Trevor advance notice that he would be
answering a question after we read the next paragraph.

The vocation of teaching—like all vocations—is a call and a
discipline. The grace that Katy rediscovered in her prayer did not *changes*
make the tasks of her day any less difficult; rather, that grace made *perception*
not
her more aware, more attentive, more patient, and more intentional. *actions*
In the refreshing silence of the Blessed Sacrament, that which Katy
always "knew" to be true became at once the gift of confirmation
and the challenge of mission: you are loved into being; now go love
others into being.

Not unlike the prophet Elijah whose frustration and desperation
drove him to Mount Horeb, Katy was first received in peace and then
empowered to "go, return on your way" (1 Kgs 19:15, RSV). For
Katy, this sending back was into the concrete realities of her vocation,

to the very same students with whom frustration had been growing. What changed in Katy was the way she saw those trying days and the students who tested her patience: she began to see these encounters anew as opportunities to love. The mystery of grace tends to go this way: not reducing the challenges of life in the world but making you capable of being more loving. At the end of the school year, Katy exercised new creativity for the discipline of teaching.

Story 9: "Waiting for Gabriel" by Timothy O'Malley

For this final story, I will forgo offering the context for the narrative and instead record more of the words from the storyteller himself, Tim O'Malley, who shared the story from which these excerpts come in the October 22, 2012, issue of *America* magazine:

> When my wife and I were first married, . . . the priest prayed over us: "Bless them with children and help them to be good parents. May they live to see their children's children." In our first year of marriage in Boston, we decided it was time to begin a family. Month one passed. Month two. Month three. Six months later, our home became the anti-Nazareth as we awaited an annunciation that never came. The hope-filled decision to conceive a child became a bitter task of disheartened waiting. After a year, we began to see infertility specialists, who concluded that we should be able to have a child. No low sperm counts. No problems with either of our reproductive systems. The verdict: inexplicable infertility. . . .
>
> The aftermath of the diagnosis was painful for both of us. It affected not simply our friendships and our own relationship but also our spiritual lives. Our infertility gradually seeped into our life of prayer. Every morning, I rise and ask God for a child. I encounter the chilly silence of a seemingly absent God. Early on I found consolation in the

language of the Psalms: "My God, My God, why have you abandoned me?" (Ps 22:2). Like the psalmist, I had my "enemies": the friendly priest who, upon learning that Kara and I do not have children, made it a point to say each time he saw me, "No children, right?"; [and] the Facebook feed filled with announcements of pregnancies and births, a constant reminder of our empty nest. Even God became my nemesis: Why have you duped me, O Lord? Why us? We have given our lives to you, and our reward is pain and suffering. . . .

As I have learned most of all through the Eucharist, Kara and I were not married for ourselves. We were married that our lives might become an offering of love for the world. For our nieces, for our nephews, for a child not biologically our own but whom we hope one day to welcome. Even our infertility is not about us. It's about how God can transform our sorrow into joy, how even in the shadow of this cross, the light shines in the darkness and the darkness will not overcome it. Of course, our woundedness remains. But prayer has given it a shape, a reason, a participation in God's very life. Even through this suffering, the Word desires to become flesh in my life through a prayerful obedience to the will of a God whom I cannot quite comprehend. . . . So we stand waiting for Gabriel, learning to hear the angel's voice in new ways: in time spent with our godchildren, in signing up to serve as foster parents, in delighting in each other's presence. And the more I enter into the grace of prayer, the more I see that Gabriel has already come in these moments: *Let it be done to me according to your word.*

I wonder if we might think about this story as a story of absence from beginning to end. In the beginning, the absence is the advent of hopeful anticipation that soon becomes the absence of sorrow and the desolation of expectations unfulfilled. In the segments of the story not reprinted here, Tim traces the ways in which he and his wife, Kara, spoke their sorrow into prayer. He continued to recite the Psalms in daily prayer, he meditated upon crucifixes whenever he went into a church, he developed an appreciation for the silence that he heard in prayer, and he grew to recognize even more fully the Eucharistic dimensions of the Christian life. Like myself, Tim is a trained theologian, so he "knew" all these things already, but "knowing" and "testifying to" are not the same thing, and in the course of his story Tim commits himself as testament to the depths of what he learned to believe. In the depths of that belief born of suffering and practice, the absence at the heart of the story becomes something new again as something unexpected blossoms: renewed delight in godchildren and nieces and nephews, an openness to welcome through fostering those children whom others have not welcomed, and a desire for adoption. The absence never left but rather became a new openness.

And at the appointed time, the "yes" of that new openness welcomed the gift of a child. In late December of 2012—more than seven years after their nuptial blessing—Tim and Kara traveled two hours from their home to receive the gift of a single mother who gave to the world the gift of a baby boy. The joy that they themselves received they in turn gave to others, not least of which were my wife and I, who received from Tim and Kara, our beloved friends, the gift of our beloved godson. Thanks be to God.

Illumination

The pieces of stories gathered above are best described as reflections of grace. That which reflects receives and returns light coming from elsewhere, and the thing is thereby changed in the process. Light cannot be seen as it passes through empty space—light is only visible as it shines upon, through, or back from something else; otherwise, you can only see by the light but not actually see light itself. The operation of grace in the world holds to this property, yet the experiences that bear forth the light of grace also work together toward another end: all of these stories tend toward the revelation of what is truly ordinary as the real order of creation. In their own ways, these storytellers seek to reflect the presence of God whose mystery cannot be captured even as God wills to be known. The mystery of grace is never reduced as we tell stories about it; paradoxically, the mystery deepens the more we attend to how it works. Those who tell stories of grace participate in speaking about the constancy of God's light across the immense diversity of life experiences. In the words of C. S. Lewis, "The Glory flows into everyone, and back from everyone: like light and mirrors. But the light's the thing."[13]

The practice of observing and speaking about grace promotes both sensitivity to its presence and fluency in its language. Becoming a dialogue partner with God in the order of grace changes you. Like light passing through a prism or stained glass, grace makes the one who speaks its words more vibrant, more defined, and more complex. Clichés cannot account for this thickness of being, nor can merely empirical observations. Grace draws its recipients into a deeper and richer engagement with life and facilitates the growth necessary to testify to the meaning of this life lived in the presence of God. To learn to speak of grace is to testify to a God who is personally invested in the world, who knows us, loves us, and calls us forth into the fullness of life in Christ. Seeing the world in this way and speaking in these terms changes everything, beginning with the imagination. This transformation is so complete that even at the end of all learning and speaking, the simple mystery of the complexity of grace leaves us with an almost inexplicable sense of gratitude for something we have experienced but cannot fully comprehend. Even when all the stories are told, the storytellers find themselves in a state of wonder not unlike Saint Thomas Aquinas who, even with all his sophisticated treatises, finds himself awestruck, perplexed, and delighted in the presence of grace:

> When you recognize her beauty,
> the eye applauds, the heart stands in ovation,
> and the tongue when she is near
> is on her best behavior,
> it speaks more like light.

> What does light talk about?
> I asked a plant once.

> It said, "I am not sure,
> but it makes me
> grow."[14]

Chapter 4

Catching Up to the Speed of Light

Forging Communion through Regular Practices

Loneliness is the most serious hidden ailment in modern life. By now, it almost goes without saying that the more we are connected technologically and commercially, the less we know each other. When social media can deliver the curated summaries of each individual life—often manicured to please and elicit admiration—the incentive to patiently listen to one another diminishes. We know so many things about each other without really knowing each other well. On the flip side, we say so much without going through the hard work of honestly sharing ourselves through what we say and how we say it. As the capacity to share ourselves with each other wanes, our gatherings in both virtual and actual space become more the coincidence of mutual loneliness than of authentic community.[1] The good news within the bad is that the desire for community and a sense of belonging endures even when the means for fulfilling these desires are misdirected or faulty. As balm for the wound of loneliness, the arduous and liberating practice of sharing and receiving stories of grace teaches us, little by little, how to become fully human together.

Dorothy Day knew this illness and its cure without ever having to consult sociological or psychological research: she experienced the ailment of loneliness in herself and in the poor. The urge to separate from each other—catalyzed by the industrial, technological, or economic forces of depersonalization that induce such separations—drives us away from our common good.[2] To share life with each other is the good for which we were all created. In the postscript to her autobiography, *The Long Loneliness*, Day speaks plainly and eloquently to the healing that community brings, beginning quite simply with conversation:

> We were just sitting there talking when lines of people began to form, saying, "We need bread." We could not say, "Go, be thou filled." If there were six small loaves and a few fishes, we had to divide them. There was always bread.
>
> We were just sitting there talking and people moved in on us. Let those who can take it, take it. Some moved out and that made room for more. And somehow the walls expanded. . . .
>
> We cannot love God unless we love each other, and to love each we must know each other. We know Him in the breaking of bread, and we know each other in the breaking of bread, and we are not alone any more. Heaven is a banquet and life is a banquet, too, even with a crust, where there is companionship.
>
> We have all known the long loneliness and we have learned that the only solution is love and that love comes with community.[3]

What Dorothy Day came to understand is that we do not first know ourselves and then enter into community; instead, we only come to truly know ourselves in and through community. This mystery of knowing and of being known always begins in God's act of making himself known through entering into communion with us in the whole sweep of salvation history culminating in the Incarnation. This divine act opens up the possibility for us to come to know one another through the grace of sharing life together in Christ. We break bread together; we receive the gift of companionship, and we share this gift in sharing our lives with one another, in the mutual exchange of receiving and giving. Whenever it is difficult to believe that "God is a personal being involved in the lives of people today,"[4] practicing communion with one another creates the conditions for us to better apprehend God's abiding presence—not first intellectually but personally.

My wager is that the practice of sharing stories of grace is a way of "sharing bread" whereby what nourishes one person may, in turn, nourish others. Geoffrey Burdell, whose story I shared in part in the previous chapter, witnessed to this life-giving grace when he discovered companionship in the midst of his own isolation in suffering. The openness of others to share their stories and Geoff's willingness to receive what others offered him turned a situation of emptiness into a fruitful new beginning. When we become givers and receivers of stories of grace, we practice a form of communion that helps cure loneliness, "and we are not alone any more."[5]

In this last full chapter, I will offer suggestions for how to incorporate the sharing of stories of grace in various pastoral and educational settings with the explicit hope of encouraging this form of witness as a regular part of the life of faith communities. Exchanging stories is a way of building authentic community: through this practice we come to know each other and, even more, to understand the mystery of grace in our lives and in the world. The hard and patient work of crafting a story forces the storyteller to take responsibility for being someone—specifically, for being one who is known in the mercy of God and for making oneself

known to others by that light. To receive such a story is to begin
to assent to the order of grace that illumines the true order of
the world. As I offer suggestions and comment on models in the
following pages, it should be obvious that I am not setting out
to provide an exhaustive list of possibilities and that the limits of
my own imagination do not set the limits of the possibilities for
utilizing stories of grace to renew faith-formation efforts. Even
so, I hope that my own suggestions and comments will spur the
creativity of practitioners who are the experts in their own settings
and who can imagine far better than I what possibilities await them
and those they serve. I count as experts not only those who hold
professional titles but also those who assume the role of parent,
mentor, or lay evangelist because we all share the promise and the
task of living into and spreading the Good News of Jesus Christ.

In the suggestions and comments to follow, I think only about
the particular kind of stories with which I have been working from
the beginning, that is, the more specific and more limited stories of
grace that offer a view of one's life in the light of God from a particular experience or set of experiences but do not seek to tell the whole
of one's story at once. That being said, the possibilities that others
may imagine certainly may include the longer stories where one seeks
to tell something closer to the whole story of one's life in the light
of grace. Yet even the longer and more comprehensive stories must,
if they are to speak well of grace, build upon the same principles as
the shorter stories. Beginning with seeing the particular well helps
you move toward understanding the whole, as when you enter a new
space with different light and allow your vision to come into focus
by gazing first at one particular feature of the place before seeing
everything together. Overgeneralization constantly threatens our perceptivity to grace, but broadening the scope of a story should never
reduce the importance of the particular and the concrete. Rather, the
work of broadening a view entails connecting and expanding upon

what is perceived in and understood about the concrete particulars. This commitment to the particular is essential to the fulfillment of the desire to know and be known. Telling our stories of grace teaches us to know ourselves as people who are first of all known in the love of God, and sharing these stories with one another permits us to know each other more fully and with humility. If there is a special need and a special opportunity for renewing evangelization efforts with emerging adults, then we should not only fill but also surround that life stage with disciples who practice sharing stories of grace that deepen belief and form identity. The mutual exchange of stories of grace is a mark of a grace-filled community.

Reimagining Sacramental Formation: A Proposal for Confirmation, RCIA, and Marriage Preparation

As I stated in chapter 1, fashioning our lives as stories of grace is the aim of Christian formation, and so this book is about Christian formation without being about *all* of Christian formation. Crafting and sharing stories of grace is an important dimension and skill of the larger aim, and the practice of storytelling stands alongside other dimensions and skills of formation. In like manner, more intentionally incorporating stories of grace in sacramental preparation and mystagogy promises to enrich and strengthen the broader formation that the Church provides at these times without presuming to accomplish all of the work required for forming disciples for full, conscious, and active participation in the life of the Church. The practice and pedagogy of stories of grace is a part of the larger task of Christian formation.

   In particular, the formation for Confirmation and the Rite of Christian Initiation of Adults (RCIA) are ideal occasions for utilizing stories of grace since these stories invite and even demand that those being formed in the Catholic faith practice articulating their faith. As noted previously, deficient articulacy in matters of faith is one of the most significant impediments to growth in religious identity; therefore, promoting religious articulacy and the abilities for testifying to faith are key objectives for holistic formation.[6] Formation for Confirmation and RCIA are also ideal because they require practicing disciples to accompany those who are being formed for lifelong discipleship. As such, these periods of formation are privileged opportunities for establishing a form of communion that aids the growth in faith of all involved.

One model for incorporating stories of grace in a dynamic way within Confirmation/RCIA formation entails each sponsor/godparent crafting a story of grace, perhaps first in written form. The pastoral team (or director of religious education [DRE]) would of course need to prepare and guide the sponsors/godparents in this task, likely beginning with a brief orientation session at the start of the period of formation. In order to explain what these stories of grace are like, it would be helpful for the pastoral team to provide examples and offer a brief training utilizing the guiding principles elucidated in this book (see especially chapter 2). The sponsors/godparents then meet with the pastoral team again to share these stories or otherwise give them to the team as written stories. For the remainder of the year of formation, the pastoral team then invites certain sponsors/godparents to share their stories during formational sessions with those preparing to receive the sacraments. The written stories may also be shared directly with the person each sponsor/godparent is guiding, especially if there is not an opportunity for every sponsor/godparent to share their story with the group. If a story or two is shared once or even twice a month, the new disciples will benefit both from the glimpses of grace that these stories provide and from the witness of more mature disciples who model how to take grace seriously in one's life and share testimonies of that grace with others.

In response to this facet of formation, the newly confirmed will then craft their own stories of grace during the mystagogical period of formation. These stories may then be shared with the group with whom they have been preparing as well as with families or other members of the community who would attend storytelling sessions, perhaps within the context of a larger formational session or prayer service. Furthermore, the pastoral team may choose to include written stories from the newly confirmed—as well as from the sponsors/godparents—in a printed (or digital) collection that the newly confirmed and their sponsors receive as a gift from the parish (or school). The stories will thus stand as symbols of an entire formational process and as a testament to the light of grace by which both the newly confirmed and the more experienced disciples are learning to see all things. It is important to stress, however, that these stories are *not* intended to be the entire story of one's life of faith; rather, these stories should be specific and relate to distinct episodes or experiences. The real benefit comes from the practice of learning to see grace well and speak of grace in particular ways rather than trying to say everything all at once.

A similar approach is possible for marriage preparation. Without becoming too idiosyncratic, particular stories from married life may be shared for the benefit of those preparing for marriage. Again, the purpose is not to try to say everything there is to say about marriage, nor need there be a concern with trying to say the most important things through these stories. These stories are also not supposed to be occasions for giving advice or recommending best practices. Instead, speaking with clarity and in compelling narrative form about the specific experiences, encounters, and even challenges of married life offers a benefit to those entering into the sacrament that is distinct from other elements of preparation and, hopefully, ongoing formation.

For example, I once had an older friend of mine who shared a particular part of his family's story with me. His teenage son had recently been diagnosed with schizophrenia, and he shared the story of his family's journey with me briefly but powerfully. What my friend said toward the end of the story has shaped the way in which I think of my own vocation as a husband and a father, and I think about these words often (in fact, I memorized them): "I ask for your prayers for our son and for our family. This is not a path we would have chosen, yet it is our path, and God says that it is holy. We are trying to do our part to make it so." Both my friend and I could write long essays on why this kind of familial love as a response to suffering is truly Christian and expressive of the vocation of marriage. What persuaded me and moved me, though, was my friend's *story*—his living witness—that gave this belief flesh in a particular set of circumstances with the members of his family. He did not share everything about his life, but in sharing this one story he shared himself, his faith, and his hope with me, who, as a younger husband and father, stood to benefit from the wisdom of his experience. I have not always remembered the advice people have offered to me over the years, and I rarely remember lectures on how to be a good husband and father, but I will never forget my friend's story. His story opened up a realm of belief for me that was not previously attainable, and I am forever grateful.

If marriage preparation can assist couples in learning to attend to the concrete particulars of the life of grace and learn to speak about them with clarity and wonder, that will help spouses to develop important skills for knowing each other well and practicing communion in their life together. It is not uncommon for anxiety in married life to grow because of a generalized concern for the grand narrative of the marriage, worrying about everything all at once rather than learning how to first abide together in the concrete particulars, to share struggles and joy together in these particulars.

Giving more experienced couples the responsibility of crafting stories of grace from their marriage—either together or separately—provides a model for those entering into marriage on how to practice the life of grace with attentiveness and simple wonder. Moreover, the challenge of crafting these stories is an opportunity for ongoing formation for the more experienced spouses themselves. As with the previous proposal, there is an opportunity here for continuing formation sessions with the newly married couple where they might, in turn, share stories of grace with other newly married couples and, ideally, with the mentor couples too. There is an almost embarrassing simplicity to all of this, but this simplicity is not unlike what Dorothy Day recognized as the consistent practices that forged bonds of communion in the Catholic Worker, that is, the practices of conversation and breaking bread together.

Reimagining Retreat Ministry: A Proposal for Introducing New Norms for High School and College Life

Faith formation is best when it is consistent, coherent, and integrated. This is true for Confirmation, RCIA, and marriage preparation, though, especially for the latter, formation is often condensed into more isolated events such as retreats. In some cases, this also occurs in high schools and colleges, where the majority of a school's faith formation might occur over specific weekends that are not necessarily contextualized within a larger framework. While the best retreats are typically those that are part of a larger formational curriculum, even when a retreat stands as a "one-off" event, the promise for renewing or even changing ways of seeing and modalities of belief are precious. All but two of the stories from which excerpts were taken in the previous chapter were shared at one of the five-day summer retreats (or conferences) of Notre Dame Vision. Some of the participants who received those stories in their oral forms were attending the retreat in continuity with the larger ministerial designs of a sponsoring Catholic institution (parish, diocese, or high school), while others attended the retreat without a formal connection to a broader effort. In either case, the participants benefitted from the glimpses of grace and the models for how to craft and share such stories. For some, a certain story's topic resonated closely with their own life experiences, and they thus found both a form of accompaniment and a guide for how to seek grace within their own experiences. For others, when the experiences shared did not match up with their own life experiences in obvious ways, what they received was the witness of those who have practiced seeing and speaking of grace as an act of faith and were therefore implicitly encouraged and challenged as listeners to do the same. Regardless of the circumstances, receiving the stories of others is a way of encountering other people as they are on the terms they allow grace to provide. The exchange of speaking and listening is a bond of communion that draws persons together.

Following from the core proposals shared about in regard to Confirmation and RICA that were then extended to a consideration for marriage formation, a process for turning story recipients into storytellers is also possible for retreat participants. Follow-up gatherings may be planned for retreatants to offer ongoing formation and fellowship during which they themselves share stories of grace with one another. A lunchtime prayer service or evening vespers are simple and appropriate occasions for one or more former retreat participants to practice sharing their own stories with their peers. In addition to affording those who once received stories to now take on the role of giving, the community as a whole benefits from the practice of listening well to who others really are, which, especially in a high school setting, goes a long way toward dispelling the often pervasive stereotypes and assumptions that accrue to various individuals.

If the practice of sharing stories of grace becomes regular within a community, then the need for creating special conditions for these stories to be shared becomes less necessary. Once a community becomes acquainted with the practice, shorter and less elaborate prayer gatherings or "mini-retreats" become more than apt occasions for the sharing of stories. Imagine, for instance, if a Catholic high school that already runs a set of retreats began extending the work initiated in those retreats through ongoing gatherings for sharing stories of grace, with the practice becoming so regular within the community that the sessions that were once follow-ups were capable of standing on their own. Not only would the retreat program be strengthened since the school developed a way to extend the benefit of the retreat into the rest of the school year, but also the school's campus ministry would enhance its pastoral reach relative to even those who do not partake in the retreats. In school environments where many wounds develop because of lack of understanding between students and the misperceptions that exist among them, the regular practice of listening to and learning from one another has the potential for important healing on behalf of personal and communal growth. Again, in regard to a high school setting, this communal practice would form teenagers who are themselves on the cusp of the critical emerging adult period and who, therefore, would take the experience, desire, and skills of knowing and being known into that coming phase of development.

In the college setting in which I teach and work, one of the residence hall communities sets up small discussion groups following the school's orientation weekend for the benefit of its new first-year students. Upperclassmen leaders join these first-year students to give them the opportunity to enter into authentic conversation with one another and their elder dorm mates after absorbing a tremendous amount of information during orientation and while immersed in a significant period of transition as they adjust to their new setting.

I wonder if small groups such as these that form right at the outset of college life, for example, might become not only regular communities for conversation but also occasions for sharing stories of grace. What if these groups met once a month for an hour each time, during which they shared prayer together and engaged in some topical conversation (or open conversation), while each time one or two upperclassmen and eventually the younger students too shared a story of grace with the group? With the right instruction and discipline, each story would only take five to eight minutes, but the long-term value of this practice of regularly sharing and receiving stories would subtly but significantly change the texture of how the members of the group know and are known by each other. As with the idea of extending retreats that I mentioned above, the objective here would be to make the practice of sharing stories of grace more regular, more common, and thus more formative for how members of a community perceive themselves and one another in God's light.

Reimagining Parish Life: A Proposal for Enriching the Meaning of "Faith Community"

Parish missions serve as moments of renewal and reorientation for an entire parish community. When my own parish hosted a weekend mission some years ago, several parishioners worked with the mission host to craft stories of their own to share during each mission session. The host led the longer portion of each session, and the parishioners—usually two per session—then shared a story of grace from their life that provided a particular illustration of the general theme. Among others, one parishioner's story related to his lifelong struggle with alcoholism, another told the story of his battle with colon cancer and his family's experience with his treatment and healing, while another (rather successful!) parishioner shared a story about her bouts with self-doubt and the challenges of maintaining a healthy regard for herself. I remember sensing my vision of my own parish shifting as I listened to some people whom I knew well and others whom I only knew by sight offering us an opening into their experiences of grace in real life that heretofore were unknown to me and to the rest of my fellow parishioners. In a parish as with any other regular community, we often think we know each other—or we assume we know just as much as we need or want to know—until an opportunity for receiving real stories from real people comes forth and we realize (or at least I did) that *really* knowing each other is much more demanding and much more rewarding than previously expected. Though the parish mission was, as a whole, renewing and reorienting as it was intended to be, I know I am not the only one who found the sharing of those stories to be the most precious gift of all. The odd thing is that this gift came from members of our own community, but we only shared and received those stories when someone came in from elsewhere and created the opportunity for us to do so. All those people and all those stories were already there, though we hadn't spoken and we hadn't listened to one another in this way before. This exchange of stories enriched the meaning of what it means to be a "community of faith" who worships, learns, and serves together in the Body of Christ.

Several years removed from that mission, the kind of stories that were shared then have once again settled back into the privacy of individual lives (and I am no exception). Outside of my personal friends at the parish or very public occurrences (such as long-term illnesses or deaths), I cannot remember coming to know members of my parish as well as I did on those days when stories were shared during our parish mission. Why is that? For parish communities, why not make the sharing of stories of grace a regular practice rather than something reserved for special events?

With each of the proposals I have offered thus far, I am encouraging regularity with the practice of exchanging stories of grace.

The fact of the matter, however, is that in order to take on a new regular practice, we often need to begin with some kind of irregular or special event. The period of preparation and short-term ongoing formation for Confirmation, RCIA, or marriage are the kinds of special occasions that naturally garner attention and some level of investment, while retreats in high schools, colleges, or even parishes and dioceses represent other such occasions. I have identified the parish mission in this section because it is a distinctive event that typically harnesses the energies of the entire parish, or at least aims to do so. In the absence of a parish mission, though, utilizing the rhythm of the liturgical year is another way to initiate a new regular practice of exchanging stories of grace.

Advent and Lenten faith-sharing groups and Bible study groups are prime candidates for this task since a commitment to a four- or six-week group is much more feasible than a yearlong or open-ended commitment. With an Advent group that is structured around the O Antiphons, for instance, one or two members of a group each week might craft a story that corresponds, in some measure, with one or more of the saving actions of the Lord upon whom we wait. For the Key of David (*O Clavis David*), one could tell a story of being freed from some form of bondage to sin, addiction, or false image of oneself; for Wisdom (*O Sapientia*), one could tell a story of learning prudence; and for the Dawn (*O Oriens*), one could tell the story of finding new life or new hope after an experience of death, especially the death of a loved one. In this way, the hopeful anticipation of the coming of the Lord is both revealed by fulfillment in the life of God's people and, on the basis of these, incites further longing for our final fulfillment when "God may be all in all" (1 Cor 15:28).

As for Lent, perhaps a group might engage in the study of the scriptures, such as the Songs of the Suffering Servant in Isaiah or the book of Tobit on the practice of almsgiving. The stories parents are able to tell about bearing the cost for loving their children in steadfast fidelity opens up new ways of understanding who this God is who clings to us more tenderly and more fiercely than we could even imagine our own mothers doing (see Is 49:15). The strength of parental love in particular situations amplifies the strength of the heavenly Father's love, a Father who makes haste to help us. The story my friend shared with me about his and his family's steadfast love for his son through the hardship of mental illness comes to mind again. His is a story worth sharing not only as a witness to the vocation of a parent but also as an analogy of divine love. The spectrum of meaning for the Lenten journey toward and with the Suffering Servant intensifies when the light of grace refracts through my friend's story.

With the book of Tobit, a member of my own parish (who also happens to be a renowned biblical scholar), Gary Anderson, once opened up the depth of Tobit's reliance upon the economy of charity with a story his wife shared with him. When he published a book on the biblical understanding of charity a few years later, he reproduced the story that he had previously told to the members of our Lenten Bible study and faith-sharing group:

> My wife was once in charge of a swimming class for adults that included a number of individuals who had had near-drowning experiences in their younger years. This naturally led to an extraordinary fear of the water. Now, anyone who has done a proper investigation of the physics of water knows that the human body is buoyant enough to float quite naturally on its surface. But in order to exploit this fact, you have to be *relaxed*, and, in turn, must *trust* the capacity of water to hold your body afloat. The more you fear the water, the more you tense up. And the more you tense up, the more you thrash about. The result? It's nearly impossible to come up for air. Because the students my wife taught had been conditioned to fear the water, they could not trust its natural capacity

for buoyancy. . . . Knowing something and acting on that
knowledge are often two quite different things.[7]

With this story, Gary was sharing with us something about the
challenge and discipline of learning to trust in divine charity that
upholds the whole world, including our own experiences of suffering
and loss. He learned about this from his wife's story, and she had
learned about this from the stories of others who had had traumatic
experiences in the water. That these people could learn to trust the
water again when they had very good reason not to illuminates for
those of us who are familiar with the consequences of sin, who are
wounded by the misdeeds of others, or who just watch the evening
news what it is like to trust in divine charity in a world that often
supports another order. The story Gary related to the members of
our group did help to teach us something, but it was not initially
shared with the purpose of teaching. It was shared as a story worth
telling, one that had become a sign of grace in his life because it was
a sign of grace in his wife's life first. This reminds me of Victoria's
story from the previous chapter, where the "theological education"
she received from her teacher occurred as she learned to trust in what
she was invited to see from her perspective as a eucharistic minister,
a position from which Victoria's faith moved toward understanding.
In like manner, the meaning of trusting in God's charity occurred in
some significant way for Gary's wife, for Gary, and finally for those
of us who received this story through the wonder of fearful people
learning to trust the buoyancy of water again.

   If Advent, Lent, or some other liturgical occasion allows groups
to form for some specific purpose, and if stories of grace are incorporated into those gatherings, then once the original objective for
the groups is fulfilled, the practice of sharing stories of grace may
well continue through other means. Perhaps the Advent or Lenten
groups gather once a month at someone's home to pray evening
prayer, enjoy dessert, and listen to someone's story of grace. The

[handwritten margin note: bad experience don't destroy the fundamental truth]

whole evening need not take more than an hour or so. Or perhaps parents or even teenagers who participated in the liturgically oriented groups are provided with resources for initiating the practice of sharing stories of grace within their own families. With a little bit of structure mixed with clear intention, the isolation of private faith lives may open up to interpersonal and communal practices of faith sharing through the exchange of stories of grace.

Reimaging Service Experiences: A Proposal for Focusing on Specific Encounters

Stories of grace offer substantial means to help students process and better grasp the importance of encounters from mission trips or service projects. The experiences from these trips and projects can have an enormous impact on those who participate, but articulacy commonly lags behind the significance of that impact. Learning to speak with precision and care about particular aspects of the experience goes a long way toward allowing the short-term impact to have long-term implications for personal and communal formation. Stories of grace do not seek to summarize or tell about the entirety of a service experience; rather, a story of grace concerns a particular encounter or a smaller experience contained within the larger one.

I think here of my friend Stephanie who, during the course of a weekend service trip to Father Greg Boyle's Homeboy Industries in downtown Los Angeles, found herself seated among migrant workers who only spoke Spanish. Her high school and college French classes were of no use to her in this company, and so this never-stop, always-on-the-go extrovert was required to rely on bilingual members of her group to translate between her dinner companions and herself. Unable to control the conversation as was her usual preference, Stephanie was forced to slow down her customary pace of interaction and, in the process, listen and speak more patiently, thoughtfully, and deliberately. Stephanie and this small community of migrant workers encountered each other in mutually uncertain terms in the liminal space that the third-party translators provided. As she tells the story, something of the precariousness, the humility, the resiliency, and the dignity of her dinner companions was made known to her in the way they and she conversed while they broke bread together. The act of identifying, crafting, and sharing this particular story was, at that point, an indelible facet of how the larger trip formed Stephanie in some significant way.

In a second story she tells from the same trip, Stephanie recasts what one might generically describe as an experience with the homeless as a unique memory of a merciful exchange. Walking along the streets known as Skid Row, a disheveled woman sitting on the curb startled Stephanie and her fellow visitors with her abrasive shouting. Stephanie was at the end of the line of the single-file walking group, and she observed that the instinctual reflex to avoid danger and uncertainty drove her group members toward the other side of the walkway, quickening their pace to flee the disturbance. Rather than walking away, Stephanie chose to walk toward the shouting woman. Stephanie knelt down next to her, placed her own hands around the woman's, and said, "Hi. My name's Stephanie. What's your name?" No sooner did the words pass by her lips than the veil of agitation lifted from the woman's face to reveal a hidden calm and serenity.

"Cassandra. My name's Cassandra."

"Cassandra, you have *beautiful* eyes," Stephanie confessed while continuing to gently clasp the woman's hands in her own.

"Why thank you. God bless you, child." And with that, Stephanie got up, returned to the back of the line of her companions who had witnessed this brief but shocking encounter, and continued walking down the road.

In telling this story, Stephanie can and does speak to the conditions of poverty on the street, but she doesn't primarily give a report or make an argument; she also does not sermonize or deliver a lesson.

Stephanie tells the story of a woman named Cassandra whose beautiful eyes she was blessed to see, of a woman who looked back into her own eyes and conferred a blessing, and of a street that is usually only ever seen as a poor grey ember but in the light of this personal encounter shined like transfiguration for those who had a little willingness to see.[8] The concrete particularity of Stephanie's story invites listeners to consider whether what might at best seem like an extraordinary but passing moment of communion might actually have been the revelation of what is truly the ordinary beauty that fear, loneliness, and rituals of separation tend to obscure. In the end, because Stephanie was challenged to tell specific stories of this immersion experience, the meaning of her encounter with the migrant workers and then with Cassandra was not covered over by foggy, hackneyed expressions such as, "It was amazing"; "The whole trip was eye-opening"; or, "It really changed how I see things." While none of those expressions would be untrue, grace is subtler and more brilliant than those lines can tell, and grace makes demands on storytellers that require them to invest something of themselves in what they offer to others through their stories.

Reimagining Teaching: A Proposal for Using Stories to Integrate Academics and "Real Life"

The academic setting may not immediately seem like the natural place for the practice of storytelling, but in the interest of educating the whole person and promoting an integrative approach to education, the challenge of crafting and sharing a story draws forth a distinctive way of thinking and reflecting. As a teacher of theology myself, I recognize the immense value in opportunities to lead my students from knowledge to understanding when it comes to the discipline of "faith seeking understanding." While it is never a requirement that students assent to faith themselves in this academic setting, I have required students to wrestle with moral or spiritual issues in their own lives through the task of composing stories as well as challenging them to learn how to speak with the language of scripture in order to utilize its symbols and grammar as a way of narrating their own life experiences. I want simply to offer two examples of assignments that I have used to offer potential models that may be adapted and revised for the uses of other teaching professionals in their own distinctive settings.

In one theology course I teach to mostly sophomores in college titled "The Character Project: Grace and Becoming Fully Human," one of the main projects of the semester is for each student to craft a story of moral or spiritual transformation from his or her own life experience. In calling this a story of "transformation," I clarify for the students that they may recognize their stories more in terms of "formation," where practices, disciplines, and habits (or lack thereof) have contributed to and continue to contribute to the development of their character, rather than what they may otherwise assume needs to be a dramatic about-turn in their lives. In crafting these stories, it happens without fail that focusing on specific episodes or a set of connected episodes is the best way for each student to tell his or her story as *a story*. The assignment corresponds with several of the stated learning objectives of the course, such as that students "develop a basic understanding of the full arc of the Christian narrative, from creation to heavenly beatitude"; "acquire the ability to articulate the qualities of grace and the complexities of human freedom"; and "explain the essential elements of character formation and apply the Christian understanding of human development to one's own life." As their teacher, I must equip them to be able to do what I am asking them to do, so this assignment comes toward the end of the semester after we have studied the course material together for some time; in other words, by the time I ask them to write this story they have been given the opportunity to grasp the arc of the Christian narrative, to study the doctrine of grace, and to examine the elements of character formation. Having acquired the knowledge necessary to craft a story in the manner I intend, my last responsibility (besides offering them assistance as they go along) is to explain to them exactly what I want them to do. Consistent with my character as an overcommunicator, I offer them a somewhat lengthy prompt that includes the following:

> The "story of moral or spiritual trans/formation" is an occasion for you to analyze your own life and the development of your own character in light of the dimensions of character formation that have been explored in the course (from readings, lectures, and class discussions). . . . In order to write this story, you must first identify the story that you want to tell, which first assumes that you believe there is a story to tell. While it seems almost too obvious to state that you would view your life as a story (and to contain stories), you should not be so quick to take this for granted. Stories do not just exist on their own; for there to be a story, you have to learn to see it, and your act of perception is part of the story itself. . . . In suggesting that the story you will tell is moral or spiritual in nature, we are following the lead of Origen of Alexandria who, in commenting on the journey of Israel, noted two intertwined dimensions of the journey of the individual soul: the first having to do with the uprightness of life (moral) and the second having to do with the accommodation to heavenly bliss (spiritual).[9] You need not explicitly clarify which kind of story you are telling—especially since the two are in fact intertwined—but rather you should use these categories as guiding lights for first identifying and then tracing your story. . . . You should take care to tell a complete story with the appropriate amount of detail (what is necessary, neither too much nor too little) and with clear evidence of the sort of theological reflection that is appropriate to the course. On this last point, *you are required to include footnotes* in your written

story that provide both commentary on and references to texts, themes, and/or discussions from the course.

Since this is not a typical academic assignment, I spill quite a lot of ink in offering instructions and spend a fair amount of time talking about the assignment in class. I also offer the students examples from some of my previous students (with their permission, of course) to show both what these stories are like and how students utilize the footnotes that allow for the explicit contact with course material. In the end, each student delivers his or her story in two ways: first, they share the story orally in class in no less than five and no more than eight minutes; second, as suggested above, each student submits a written version of the story that I read and grade and in which footnote annotations are included (this version may be slightly longer than the oral version). These annotations are not part of the story itself, and they do not provide "the meaning" of the story; rather, the annotations provide me, as the teacher, with an understanding of how the student has come to see his or her story through the education of the course. This work of academic translation and integration not only helps the students meet the learning objectives of the course but also provides them with something worth taking with them as they leave the course, since the memory of one's own story is often stronger than the memory of an essay (though I assign plenty of essays as well). Moreover, these stories are also gifts that they bestow upon one another when they share them orally so that the work and witness of others becomes part of what each student gains from the course. Needless to say, it is both difficult and gratifying to allow intellectual growth to illumine life experience, so there is often ample concern about this assignment beforehand and abundant gratitude (and relief!) when it is complete.

The second assignment, designed by my colleague Tim O'Malley (whose story appeared in the previous chapter), comes from a course that Tim and I coteach, titled "The Christian Experience: Vocation and the Theological Imagination."[10] As a whole, the course aims to "provide an entrée into the theological foundations of Christian vocation through considering the transformation of human experience by means of the theological imagination." One of the explicit learning objectives of the course is for each student to "become practiced in perceiving one's own narrative through the themes of the Christian imagination," which follows directly upon two of the other course objectives: "explore the images and narratives of salvation that are the foundation of Christian vocation" and "cultivate an understanding of Catholic doctrine as a way of life, one transformative of human experience." After several weeks spent diagnosing the modern secular imagination and then attending closely to the Apostles' Creed as a symbol of revelation and summary of Christian doctrine, we lead the students through examples of the creativity of the Christian imagination, both ancient and modern, beginning with a close reading of Saint Augustine's *Confessions*. A central lesson from this text is the way in which Augustine's own imagination is healed and redeemed through the images and narratives of the scriptures, through which he finds the only way to "give a coherent account of [his] disintegrated self."[11] Augustine takes on the words and the life of the scriptures in order to speak his own story anew. The assignment for our students is to take one of their own life experiences and tell the story of this experience in prayer *to God* using scriptural language to do so, after Augustine's own model. In short, the students practice receiving and offering the very language that God provides in order to offer their own life experiences as a story (or potential story) of God's mercy. The instructions we give to the students are as follows:

1.   Choose a narrative within your life in which God's "re-cre-ation" of you is relatively easy to discern (or an event in which you'd like to perceive God's action within your life). The narrative need not be a matter of sin but may be a confession of

praise, a moment in which you grew to perceive the world anew.

2.   The text should be written as a prayer to God, "confessing" to God the main contours of the story. The format of prayer will reveal aspects of your narrative you've never considered before.

3.   It is necessary to incorporate images of the scriptures through the text in addition to quoting from the scriptures themselves. The images from the scriptures could structure the entire narrative. You should also introduce scriptural language throughout the text.

As with the previous assignment, students are graded on the plot, structure, and language of the narrative as well as how they incorporate theological insights and draw forward dimensions studied in our course. Notice, however, that from beginning to end these assignments call for the students to *craft a story*. They are not writing an academic paper by ordinary means, even though, at least in terms of the first assignment, they are annotating the story with academic content. Assignments such as these that challenge the students to speak in stories introduce them to different ways of knowing and often lead to depths of understanding not previously attained.

Creating Cultures of Grace

The regular practice of sharing stories of grace is a targeted response to the prevalent lack of belief in "God as a personal being involved in the lives of people today."[12] Moreover, the commitment to incorporating stories of grace into faith-formation efforts for teenagers, emerging adults, young adults, and mature adults contributes to an ordinary and consistent environment where testimonies to the action of grace shape how disciples learn to see themselves, each other, and the world around them. If a determined focus on emerging adults is vital for the work of the new evangelization in order to renew the life of the Church and form disciples in an identity born of knowing themselves in God's mercy, then the best approach will not focus on emerging adults alone. It is incumbent upon parents, pastoral ministers, and educators to form young people in such a way that when they begin to solidify their identity during their twentysomething years, they will be better prepared to do so with eyes trained for perceiving grace, with hearts open to receiving grace, and with words capable of articulating grace. In order to form young people well, it is imperative to offer substantive ongoing formation for adult disciples, including but not limited to parents and those whose professional or dedicated volunteer efforts are directed toward forming others in faith. The best way to form young people and to model faith-filled identities for emerging adults is to become adult Christians who are sensitive to, welcoming of, and fluent in the mystery of grace. The creativity of those whose work of ministry and education will invite growing disciples into the fullness of the Christian life bursts forth from both their pastoral competency and the substance of their own Christian character.

Following upon the work of the preceding chapters, I hope that this chapter contributes to a conversation among ministers and educators, as well as parents and disciples in all walks of life, toward the end of collaborating in response to the call of the Gospel in our contemporary situation. While the commitment to intentionally crafting, sharing, and receiving stories of grace certainly does not respond to every need in the Church today or to every need of emerging adults, the more we practice this art together the more we will guide each other and those whom we are called upon to educate into the realms of belief where we slowly learn to see all things in light of God's mercy. Though we cannot and should not want to control the outcome of practicing this art, we may trust, in faith, that this personal and communal commitment will lead us into becoming a more grace-filled people with the capacity to wonder at creation. To learn to see the world in grace is to know that we are never alone because each of us is the "one who is looked upon by the Lord."[13] In the light of his gaze, we find each other, "and we are not alone any more."[14] That's the good news we should tell stories about and commit to memory.

Epilogue
The Stories We Tell Ourselves

D isciples learn to see in response to being seen in mercy, and disciples learn to know all things in response to being known in the love of God. At the outset of this book, the example of Pope Francis introduced us to the paradoxical way in which a disciple learns to recognize himself: according to the light of God that breaks upon him. A disciple's identity crisis is the lifelong project of keeping first things first, and the first thing of all is that all the truth, beauty, and goodness of life depends on that singular, marvelous gift: God first loved us (1 Jn 4:19).

For disciples as much as anyone else, there are myriad other ways in which we are tempted, time and again, to primarily define ourselves. More subtle than all the stories we tell each other, more potent than all the stories that surround us on a day-to-day basis, and more elusive than the stories we would *like* to tell ourselves are the stories we *actually* tell ourselves. It is easier to diagnose and correct misguided stories in children, a little more difficult but still fairly straightforward in teenagers, rather tricky and even hazardous when working with emerging or young adults, and, in the end, incredibly difficult to reform or rebuild self-identifying stories with mature adults. While it is not quite right to say that "practice makes perfect," with respect to the stories that we tell ourselves over and over again, we would not be far off in saying practice makes *certain*. Nothing is so difficult to dislodge as settled certainty, which in this case means that the stories we practice telling ourselves become increasingly important in each stage of life. It is more difficult to begin allowing yourself to be identified primarily in the light of God's grace after the critical period that sociologists refer to as "emerging adulthood" than it is before that period.

Reflecting upon her work in clinical psychology with twenty-somethings, Meg Jay discloses that at the base of each of her clients' identity is the story or set of stories that this person tells himself or herself:

> There is a stereotype that psychologists are only interested in childhood memories. Childhood is important, but more and more I am curious about what went on in high school. High school and our twenties are not only the time when we have our most self-defining experiences[;] study after study shows they are also the time when we have our most self-defining *memories*.
>
> Adolescence is a time of many firsts, including our first attempt to form life stories. As we become capable of—and interested in—abstract thought, we start to put together stories about who we are and why. As our social networks expand across our teens and twenties, we repeat these stories to others and to ourselves. We use them to feel a sense of coherence as we move from place to place.
>
> The stories we tell ourselves become facets of our identity. They reveal our unique complexity. All at once, they say something about friends, family, and culture. They say something about *why* we live as we do from year to year. . . .
>
> The power of untold personal stories is that . . . they can loop silently in our minds without anyone, sometimes even ourselves, knowing about them. . . . Yet these stories are the bits of identity with perhaps the greatest potential for change. . . . Life stories with themes of ruin can trap us. Life stories that are triumphant can transform us. So part of what I do with clients is help them tell their stories. Then we change them.[1]

Helping people "change their stories" sounds odd at first. My own instinctual reaction is to think that this is some kind of manipulation, since a person's story is what it is and asking her or him to change that story is leading that person away from honesty. When I sit with this idea longer, however, I remember that telling a story is not reducible to the factual details the storyteller recalls because *how* the storyteller sees this experience is an expression of who the storyteller *is*. While it is true that experiences are in some measure formative of personal character, it is equally true that how we learn to see our experiences is expressive of personal character. If we look back to the stories contained within chapter 3, we witness how stories that first seemed bound for expressing abandonment, shame, emptiness, and frustration opened up as stories expressing companionship, solidarity, abundance, and deep consolation. In large part, the facts did not change; rather, the way of seeing changed. Suffering did not go away, but it was transformed; confusion was not dispelled, but it was balanced on trust. The storytellers learned to see themselves in the light of grace because they learned to recognize the signs of grace within their own lives. In telling their stories, they testified to a shift in what provided coherence to their "ordinary" lives. Those who learn to tell stories of grace subject the stories they tell themselves to being changed.

As parents, my wife and I are keenly invested in forming our children so that the stories that "loop" in their minds are shaped according to being loved, being generous, and being merciful. As a teacher of and mentor to college students, I regularly accompany late teen and early twentysomething emerging adults in confirming, reforming, and sometimes completely recasting the stories they habitually practice telling themselves. As an adult Catholic, I know all too well how difficult it is to break from the limiting or unhealthy stories I have rehearsed over and over again—stories about the need for approval, the competition for prestige, the metrics of success, and the excuses for not developing a merciful and generous character. As an adult, then, I know both how difficult and how important the challenge of telling stories of grace is for someone such as myself, which encourages me to take my work with teenagers and twenty-somethings more seriously while also refreshing me in my vocation as a parent, knowing full well how crucial the formation my wife and I provide our children is for both who they are now and who they will become later. In different ways for each stage of life, the salutary practice of crafting and telling stories of grace helps all disciples to more fully identify themselves, first and foremost, as those who are "looked upon by the Lord."[2] Refusing to trap God in the confines of their life experiences, those who practice sharing stories of grace make their life experiences transparent to the light of our merciful Lord, "in [whom] we live and move and have our being" (Acts 17:28).

Notes

1. The Light by Which We See

1. "A Big Heart Open to God: The Exclusive Interview with Pope Francis," Antonio Spadaro, *America*, September 30, 2013, http://americamagazine.org/pope-interview.

2. For more on learning to see in the light of the Resurrection, see Benedict XVI, *Jesus of Nazareth, Part II: Holy Week; From the Entrance into Jerusalem to the Resurrection* (San Francisco: Ignatius Press, 2011), esp. 241–77; and Rowan Williams, *Resurrection: Interpreting the Easter Gospel* (New York: Pilgrim Press, 1984), esp. 68–90.

3. Robert Barron, *And Now I See: A Theology of Transformation* (New York: Crossroad Publishing, 1998), 1.

4. Nicolette Manglos-Weber and Christian Smith, "Understanding Former Young Catholics: Findings from a National Study of American Emerging Adults," National Survey of Youth and Religion, University of Notre Dame, Institute for Church Life and Center for Study of Religion and Society, https://icl.nd.edu/assets/170517/icl_former_catholics_final_web.pdf, 8.

5. Jeffrey Jensen Arnett, *Emerging Adulthood: The Winding Road from the Late Teens through the Twenties*, 2nd ed. (New York: Oxford University Press, 2015), 24; see also Jeffrey Jensen Arnett, "Emerging Adulthood(s): The Cultural Psychology of a New Life Stage," in *Bridging Cultural and Developmental Approaches to Psychology: New Syntheses in Theory, Research, and Policy*, ed. Lene Arnett Jensen (New York: Oxford University Press, 2011), 255–75.

6. Arnett, *Emerging Adulthood*, 26. For further introduction to emerging adulthood, see Christian Smith et al., *Young Catholic America: Emerging Adults In, Out of, and Gone from the Church* (New York: Oxford University Press, 2014), 4–8.

7. For a book length argument supporting the importance of this decade of life in contemporary American culture, see Meg Jay, *The Defining Decade: Why Your Twenties Matter—and How to Make the Most of Them Now* (New York: Twelve, 2013).

8. Christian Smith, *Soul Searching: The Religious and Spiritual Lives of American Teenagers* (New York: Oxford University Press, 2005), 162–65.

9. Ibid., 191.

10. Kenda Creasy Dean, *Almost Christian: What the Faith of Our Teenagers Is Telling the American Church* (New York: Oxford University Press, 2010), 12.

11. Smith, *Soul Searching*, 131 (emphasis in original text).

12. "Expectant Parents Throw Some Values Together at Last Minute," *The Onion*, March 10, 2014, http://www.theonion.com/article/expectant-parents-throw-some-values-together-at-la-35482.

13. Manglos-Weber and Smith, "Understanding Former Young Catholics," 8.

14. Smith et al., *Young Catholic America*, 268–69; see also Christian Smith, *Souls in Transition: The Religious and Spiritual Lives of Emerging Adults* (New York: Oxford University Press, 2009), esp. 279–300.

15. Manglos-Weber and Smith, "Understanding Former Young Catholics," 6–7. In fact, more than 57 percent of former Catholic emerging adults still believe in God, while 24 percent are unsure, and only 19 percent no longer believe in God.

16. C. S. Lewis, "Meditation in a Toolshed," in *God in the Dock* (Grand Rapids, MI: Eerdmans, 2014), 230.

17. Marilynne Robinson, *Gilead* (New York: Picador, 2006), 14–15.

18. Ibid., 245–46.

19. Ibid., 210.

20. Flannery O'Connor, *Mystery and Manners: Occasional Prose*, ed. Sally Fitzgerald and Robert Fitzgerald (New York: Farrar, Straus and Giroux, 1969), 165. Her Thomistic influence is on display in only the most thinly veiled terms in one of her early short stories, "A Temple of the Holy Ghost," in *The Complete Stories* (New York: Farrar, Straus and Giroux, 1971) 236–48. As her skill as a writer grew, the Thomistic influence became even more embedded in her writing, and therefore it became at once more prevalent and less starkly apparent in comparison to this particular story.

21. Flannery O'Connor, "Revelation," in *The Complete Stories* (New York: Farrar, Straus and Giroux, 1971) 488–509.

22. "Flannery O'Connor," PBS, *Religion and Ethics NewsWeekly*, aired November 20, 2009, http://www.pbs.org/video/1915701265/.

23. Compare this to the chapter titled "Talking to a Stranger" in Rowan Williams, *Resurrection: Interpreting the Easter Gospel* (New York: Pilgrim Press, 1984), 68–90.

24. Manglos-Weber and Smith, "Understanding Former Young Catholics," 14–17.

25. Ibid., 14.

26. For a more expansive treatment of the modern crisis in ways of knowing in regard to the possibility of religious knowledge, see the first chapter of my forthcoming work, *Work of Love: A Theological Reconstruction of the Communion of Saints* (Notre Dame, IN: University of Notre Dame Press, 2017).

27. John Henry Newman, *An Essay in Aid of a Grammar of Assent* (Notre Dame, IN: University of Notre Dame Press, 1979), 90–91 (emphasis in original text).

28. John Henry Newman, *Apologia Pro Vita Sua*, ed. A. Dwight Culler (Boston: Houghton Mifflin, 1956), 169; cf. David S. Cunningham, *Faithful Persuasion: In Aid of a Rhetoric of Christian*

Theology (Notre Dame, IN: University of Notre Dame Press, 1991), 173–74.

29. Newman, *A Grammar of Assent*, 90.

30. See Austen Ivereigh, *The Great Reformer: Francis and the Making of a Radical Pope* (New York: Henry Holt, 2014), 310.

31. Newman, *A Grammar of Assent*, 50.

32. Robinson, *Gilead*, 240.

33. Francesca Murphy, *God Is Not a Story: Realism Revisited* (Oxford: Oxford University Press, 2007), 44.

34. See Karl Rahner, "The Eternal Significance of the Humanity of Jesus for Our Relationship with God," in *Theological Investigations*, trans. Cornelius Ernst et al., vol. 3 (Limerick, Ireland: Mary Immaculate College, 2000), 43.

35. Joseph Cardinal Ratzinger, "Pro Eligendo Romano Pontifice," homily, conclave, St. Peter's Basilica, Vatican City, April 18, 2005, http://www.vatican.va/gp11/documents/homily-pro-eligendo-pontifice_20050418_en.html

2. Bending Light

1. In a sermon on Genesis 32:10 for the celebration of Christmas, John Henry Newman expresses the priority of God's gift giving in this way: "We are not our own, any more than what we possess is our own. We did not make ourselves; we cannot be supreme over ourselves. We cannot be our own masters. We are God's property by creation, by redemption, by regeneration. He has a triple claim upon us . . . [and] we have two duties, to be resigned and to be thankful." "Remembrance of Past Mercies," in *Selected Sermons, Prayers, and Devotions* (New York: Vintage, 1999), 204.

2. See Hans Urs von Balthasar, *Prayer*, trans. Graham Harrison (San Francisco: Ignatius Press, 1986), 67.

3. See chapter 1 and the sociological analysis of the spiritual lives of youth and emerging adults.

4. Flannery O'Connor, *Mystery and Manners: Occasional Prose*, ed. Sally Fitzgerald and Robert Fitzgerald (New York: Farrar, Straus and Giroux, 1969), 112.

5. For an account of sincerity without reference to the objectivity of truth, see Harry Frankfurt, *On Bullshit* (Princeton, NJ: Princeton University Press, 2005), 67.

6. Hans Urs von Balthasar expresses the importance of this well when he writes, "For every genuine encounter with the word presupposes an accepting and receptive consent on man's part" (*Prayer*, 71). The speaking—with personality—is a part of the act of reception and, as it were, the free ratification of the offer of grace on the part of the recipient. The Spirit communicates the gift of Christ and prepares the recipient's heart to receive and respond.

7. Jeffrey Fiskin and Remi Aubuchon, "Galileo Was Right," *From the Earth to the Moon*, episode 10, directed by David Carson (HBO, aired May 3, 1998).

8. I will discuss academic assignments such as this in chapter 4.

9. I will speak to this challenge more extensively in principles 2 and 3 next.

10. O'Connor, *Mystery and Manners*, 162–63.

11. "On Writing," Kate DiCamillo, accessed October 19, 2015, http://www.katedicamillo.com/onwrit.html.

12. Simone Weil, *Awaiting God: A New Translation of "Attente de Dieu" and "Lettre à Un Religieux,"* trans. Bradley Jersak (Maywood, CT: Fresh Wind Press, 2013), 10.

13. We recall here the illustration of grace that Marilynne Robinson provides in *Gilead*, as treated in chapter 1 of this work, where a willingness and courageousness to see—a prevenient grace and a prevenient courage—is the condition of the possibility of encountering grace at all. Marilynne Robinson, *Gilead* (New York: Picador, 2006).

14. See the discussion of grace in relation to C. S. Lewis's "Meditation in a Toolshed" in chapter 1 of this work. C. S. Lewis, "Meditation in a Toolshed," in *God in the Dock* (Grand Rapids, MI: Eerdmans, 2014).

15. This is the very phenomenon that Saint Augustine probes in the enigmatic tenth book of his *Confessions*. What matters there as here is not just what there is to see but rather the light by which one sees.

16. Examples of particular expressions of grace are provided in chapter 3.

17. "A Big Heart Open to God: The Exclusive Interview with Pope Francis," Antonio Spadaro, *America*, September 30, 2013, http://americamagazine.org/pope-interview.

18. D. T. Niles, *That They May Have Life* (New York: Harper and Brothers, 1951), 96.

19. Robinson, *Gilead*, 15.

20. O'Connor, *Mystery and Manners*, 162; see also 169–210.

21. In the interest of full disclosure, I must confess that I once asked Marilynne Robinson if she was in fact communicating directly with her reader in that particular excerpt, "kissing our hands," to have us take notice just as John Ames was kissing his father's hand to draw his attention to the light. She said that her only intention in writing that scene was to tell the story and not to say something to the reader. Of course, I fully accept her response, and yet I cannot help but think that, at least functionally, that scene communicates something from author to reader in a manner similar to how John is communicating with his father.

22. "Holy Ones, Loved Ones: The Journey from All Saints to All Souls," Leonard DeLorenzo, *America*, November 2, 2015, http://americamagazine.org/issue/holy-ones-loved-ones.

23. Robinson, *Gilead*, 245.

24. For more on the "practice" of being renewed in mercy through prayer, see my "Three Steps to a Better Understanding of Mercy," *Our Sunday Visitor Catholic Publishing Company*, November 18, 2015, https://www.osv.com/OSVNewsweekly/Article/TabId/535/ArtMID/13567/ArticleID/18727/Three-steps-to-a-better-understanding-of-mercy.aspx?ref=top10.

25. Newman, "Remembrance of Past Mercies," 205.

26. Weil, *Awaiting God*, 10.

3. Speaking of Light

1. Flannery O'Connor, *Mystery and Manners: Occasional Prose*, ed. Sally Fitzgerald and Robert Fitzgerald (New York: Farrar, Straus and Giroux, 1969), 165.

2. See Augustine, *The Confessions*, trans. Maria Boulding (New York: Vintage, 1998), 147–50 (VIII.2.3–5).

3. Ibid., 147 (VIII.2.3): "To [Simplicianus] I described the winding paths of my wayward life."

4. Ibid., 153 (VIII.5.10).

5. Ibid., 168 (VIII.29); for Augustine's first reception of this story from Ponticianus, see 156 (VIII.14).

6. Ibid., 157–58 (VIII.15).

7. Ibid., 152 (VIII.4.9); cf. Acts 13:6–12.

8. Ibid., 145 (VIII.1.1).

9. Ibid., 150–51 (VIII.3.6–7); cf. Marilynne Robinson, *Gilead* (New York: Picador, 2006), 245–46.

10. L'Arche communities are homes and workplaces where people with and without intellectual disabilities live and work together as peers. Jean Vanier founded L'Arche in the mid-1960s, and these communities spread from Europe to North America and then around the world. For more information, please visit https://www.larcheusa.org/.

11. Alasdair MacIntyre, *Dependent Rational Animals: Why Human Beings Need the Virtues* (Chicago: Open Court, 1999), 2.

12. Thomas Aquinas, *Nature and Grace: Selections from the Summa Theologica of Thomas Aquinas*, ed. and trans. A. M. Fairweather, vol. 11, Library of Christian Classics (Philadelphia: Westminster Press, 2006), 165 (I–II, q. 111, a. 1, resp.).

13. C. S. Lewis, *The Great Divorce* (San Francisco: HarperOne, 2000), 86.

14. Thomas Aquinas, "What Does Light Talk About?" in *Love Poems from God: Twelve Sacred Voices from the East and West*, ed. and trans. Daniel Ladinsky (New York: Penguin, 2002), 139.

4. Catching Up to the Speed of Light

1. Tracking the changes in social interaction and the prevalence of confidants among Americans over two decades, researchers concluded that the number of intimate connections of Americans decreased significantly from the 1980s through the early 2000s (see Miller McPherson, Lynn Smith-Lovin, and Matthew Brashears, "Social Isolation in America: Changes in Core Discussion Networks over Two Decades," *American Sociological Review* 71, no. 3 [June 2006]: 353–75). This research is not without critique, as other sociological researchers question the validity of the results (see Claude Fischer, "The 2004 GSS Finding of Shrunken Social Networks: An Artifact?" *American Sociological Review* 74, no. 4 [August 2009]: 657–69). The original researchers' response to the critique of their study is available here: Miller McPherson, Lynn Smith-Lovin, and Matthew Brashears, "Models and Marginals: Using Survey Evidence to Study Social Networks," *American Sociological Review* 74, no. 4 (August 2009): 670–81. For a book-length study arguing for the correlation between increased loneliness and the rise in technologically facilitated interactions, see Sherry Turkle, *Alone Together: Why We Expect More from Technology and Less from*

Each Other (New York: Basic Books, 2012). Lastly, Elizabeth Koenig makes the sharp claim that "people lose their souls when they unconsciously commit themselves to what is in fact a shared emptiness, then try to convince themselves and the rest of the world that what they've got is community" ("Keeping Company with Jesus and the Saints," *Theology Today* 56, no.1 [April 1999]: 18). The once-Instagram star turned social media critic, Essena O'Neill, lends credence to this claim, arguing that the validation she sought through social media was not "real life" and that the disconnect between how she looked and how she felt was vast (see "Essena O'Neill Quits Instagram Claiming Social Media 'Is Not Real Life,'" Elle Hunt, *Guardian*, November 3, 2015, http:// www.theguardian.com/media/2015/nov/03/instagram-star-essena-oneill-quits-2d-life-to-reveal-true-story-behind-images). See also "7 College Students Talk About Their Instagrams and the Pressure to Seem Happy," Izzy Grinspan, *Cut*, July 31, 2015, http://nymag.com/thecut/2015/07/college-students-on-the-pressure-to-seem-happy.html. Meg Jay's chapter titled "My Life Should Look Better on Facebook" is also relevant to this point (Meg Jay, *The Defining Decade: Why Your Twenties Matter—and How to Make the Most of Them Now* [New York: Twelve, 2013], 41–54).

2. One of the best accounts of how power dissociated from personal responsibility leads to the separation of persons from one another and the loss of community in the modern world is Romano Guardini, *The End of the Modern World*, trans. Joseph Theman, Herbert Burke, and Elinor Briefs (Wilmington, DE: ISI Books, 1998), especially part 2.

3. Dorothy Day, *The Long Loneliness* (San Francisco: Harper-Collins, 1952), 285–86.

4. Nicolette Manglos-Weber and Christian Smith, "Understanding Former Young Catholics: Findings from a National Study of American Emerging Adults," National Survey of Youth and Religion,

University of Notre Dame, Institute for Church Life and Center for Study of Religion and Society, https://icl.nd.edu/assets/170517/icl_former_catholics_final_web.pdf, 8.

    5. Day, *Long Loneliness*, 286.

    6. Christian Smith, *Soul Searching: The Religious and Spiritual Lives of American Teenagers* (New York: Oxford University Press, 2005), 131.

    7. Gary Anderson, *Charity: The Place of the Poor in the Biblical Tradition* (New Haven, CT: Yale University Press, 2013), 109.

    8. Marilynne Robinson, *Gilead* (New York: Picador, 2006), 245–46.

    9. See Origen's homily 27 on Numbers, in Origen, *Homilies on Genesis and Exodus*, trans. Ronald E. Heine (Washington, DC: Catholic University of America Press, 2002), 253.

    10. The original assignment upon which this one is based comes from our common teaching mentor, Professor John Cavadini.

    11. See Augustine, *The Confessions*, trans. Maria Boulding (New York: Vintage, 1998), 25 (II.1.1).

    12. Manglos-Weber and Smith, "Understanding Former Young Catholics," 8.

    13. "A Big Heart Open to God: The Exclusive Interview with Pope Francis" Antonio Spadaro, *America*, September 30, 2013, http://americamagazine.org/pope-interview.

    14. Day, *Long Loneliness*, 286.

Epilogue

    1. Meg Jay, *The Defining Decade: Why Your Twenties Matter—and How to Make the Most of Them Now* (New York: Twelve, 2013 108–9.

    2. "A Big Heart Open to God: The Exclusive Interview with Pope Francis" Antonio Spadaro, *America*, September 30, 2013, http://americamagazine.org/pope-interview.

L eonard J. DeLorenzo teaches theology at the University of Notre Dame, where he also directs Notre Dame Vision, the Notre Dame Catechist Academy, and the Notre Dame Character Project within the Institute for Church Life. His writing has appeared in publications such as *America* and *Church Life: A Journal for the New Evangelization.*

DeLorenzo earned his doctorate in systematic theology from the University of Notre Dame, where he also earned his master's (systematic theology) and bachelor's degrees (theology and philosophy, *summa cum laude*). From August 2003 through June 2010, DeLorenzo served as the coordinator for recruitment for the Center for Catechetical Initiatives at Notre Dame. He was instrumental in creating and launching the Echo: Faith Formation Leadership Program, a graduate service program committed to renewing the ministry of catechesis in the Catholic Church. He speaks regularly on topics including the saints, adolescent catechesis, vocation and discernment, and the theological imagination.

He and his wife, Lisa, live in South Bend, Indiana, with their five children.

AVE

AVE MARIA PRESS

Founded in 1865, Ave Maria Press, a ministry of the Congregation of Holy Cross, is a Catholic publishing company that serves the spiritual and formative needs of the Church and its schools, institutions, and ministers; Christian individuals and families; and others seeking spiritual nourishment.

Handwritten notes in left margin:
Grace- Aug ← series of actions - 72
have I experienced that conversion?
will I experience that conversion?
↓
most of all, that comes through the stories of others
↓
comfort
I'm excited

For a complete listing of titles from

Ave Maria Press

Sorin Books

Forest of Peace

Christian Classics

visit www.avemariapress.com

AVE | AVE MARIA PRESS
Notre Dame, IN
A Ministry of the United States Province of Holy Cross